Egg Gravy

Authentic Recipes from the
Butter in the Well
Series

Linda K Hubalek

Egg Gravy

Authentic Recipes from the
Butter in the Well
Series

Linda K. Hubalek

Aurora, Colorado

Egg Gravy
© 1994 by Linda K. Hubalek

Second Printing 1994
Printed in the United States of America

Consulting Editor: Ione Johnson

Photos courtesy of:
Alice Bohn, Page 53.
Esther Hyrup, Pages 31, 69.
LaVern Johnson, Pages 81, 99.
Lester Johnson, Pages 52, 113.
Alice Larson, Page 50.
Nancy Olsson, Page 102.
Rozella Schaeffer, Pages v, viii, 1, 20, 24, 33, 50, 55, 73, 76, 114.

Publisher's Cataloging in Publication
    (Prepared by Quality Books Inc.)
Hubalek, Linda K.
Egg gravy: authentic recipes from the Butter in the well series
/ Linda K. Hubalek. -- 1st ed.
  p. cm. -- (Butter in the well series ; 3)
Includes index.
Preassigned LCCN: 94-76031.
ISBN 1-886652-02-3 (Previously ISBN 1-882420-10-1)

1. Cookery--Kansas. 2. Cookery, Swedish. 3. Swedish Americans --Kansas--Social life and customs. I. Title. II. Series.

TX722.S8P73 1994   641.59781'089397
                                    QB194-775

To the Women of Liberty Township

who in the past and present,
have given love, guidance and protection
to their families and community.

Standing: *Magdalena Johnson, Hannah Olson, Maria Johnson and Kajsa Runeberg.*

Sitting: *Emelia (Emily) Johnson Swenson, Emma Olson Train, Julia Runeberg Olson, Hilda Olson and Emelia (Millie) Johnson Bloomberg.*

Books by Linda K. Hubalek

Butter in the Well
Prärieblomman
Egg Gravy
Looking Back

Acknowledgments

———∙➤◄∙———

I wish to thank the people who dug into the past, and shared their memories and recipes of their ancestors with me.

I hope opening up an old ledger book or recipe box, and seeing the faded handwriting of your ancestor, has brought back warm memories. Can you close your eyes and smell the aroma of your mother's bread or angel food cake again? I hope so. That's what this book is for—to remember our favorite cooks and the food they prepared for us.

Tack så mycket.

Linda Katherine Johnson Hubalek

Special Recipes came from

Irene Akers
Louise Almquist
Mary Anderson
Emelia Bloomberg
Ellen Carlson
Lydia Carlson
Nan Clark
Ebba Forsberg
Anna Graves
Emma Hart
Anna Hyrup
Albertina Johnson
Christina Johnson
Elsie Johnson
Lillie Johnson
Maria Johnson
Magdalena Johnson
Myrtle Johnson
Freda Lindholm

Mabel Linn
Pearl Miller
Christine Nelson
Ida Nelson
Gunilla Oborg
Julia Olson
Hannah Olson
Hilda Olson
Alma Peterson
Hulda Peterson
Kristina Peterson
Alma Runneberg
Kajsa Runeberg
Hannah Shogren
Carrie Sjogren
Emelia Swenson
Gertrude Swenson
Minnie Swenson
and many others

Cream Pie.

1 heaping tablesp. Corn Starch with a [...]
[...], add ½ cup sugar, the beaten yolks [of...]
[...], and a little salt. pour this mixture in[...]
[...] of boiling milk. Pour into baked Crusts.

Cookies –

[...] Butter, 2 cups Sugar. 1 cup sour Crea[m...]
[...] 1 teasp soda. Caraway Seed.

Mince Meat –

[...] Apples, 2 lbs. Raisins, 2 lbs Currants [...]
[...] 3 cups Sugar 1 lb. Suet. 3 lbs Meat [...]
[...] Cinnamon, 3 teasp. cloves. 1½ teasp [...]
[...]ful Salt. –

Veal Loaf –

[...] veal, ¾ lbs. salt Pork, chopped fine 1 c[...]
[...] crumbs. 2 eggs 1 teasp sugar 2 teasp salt
[...] pper make into loaf and bake.

Handwritten recipes from Julia Olson's cookbook

Table of Contents

Egg Gravy. It has always been the staple meal, no matter how poor or rich we've been. No matter how low the staples were in the pantry or cellar—we always had eggs, milk and a little flour.

Egg Gravy

———◦►◄◦———

2 cups milk
2 eggs
2 tablespoons flour
salt

Heat milk. Beat eggs, flour and a little milk. When milk is hot, pour and stir the egg-flour mixture into the milk. Cook until thick. Put on toast or bread. Good served with bacon.

Introduction

—◦➤◄◦—

Faded recipes—we've all come across them from time to time in our lives—either handwritten by ourselves or by another person in our family, or as old yellowed newspaper clippings stuck in a cookbook of sorts.

While doing the research for the *Butter in the Well* series, I've found some very old recipes and home remedies. They've been handwritten in old ledger books, on scraps of paper, in margins of old cookbooks, and in the memories of the pioneer's children.

As a result, *Egg Gravy* is a collection of recipes pioneer women used during their homesteading days. They were collected from area people—family and neighbors—who had connections with Kajsa Swenson Runeberg, the main character in the book series. Some recipes I can trace back to the first generation of women who left Sweden and homesteaded in Liberty Township, Saline County in central Kansas during the 1800s. Others, I'm not sure where they originated because they've emerged from more than one person's file. At least I could tell it had been a favorite recipe passed around the neighborhood.

Although most of the recipes were written in English, some were handwritten in Swedish. Several were a combination of Swedish and English words with misspellings prominent. The immigrant women in the 1800s had very little schooling growing up in Sweden. Then they had to learn another language when they settled in America. Most of the women probably learned to read and write English when their children attended school.

When the pioneers first homesteaded on the prairie, they depended on food they could gather or hunt from the prairie. Creek and river banks were combed for wild fruit and game. When excess was available, it was dried and stored for future use. Later, when they were established on the farm, they had garden produce, fresh in the summer and preserved for the winter. Farm animals were raised and butchered for the family's meals.

Most recipes were basic, using ingredients they grew on the farm or were available at the general store. The availability of food and the season depended on when some recipes were used.

This "cookbook" is to be read, rather than used as a general book to cook from since basic instructions of how to mix ingredients, time and oven temperature are missing from the recipes. Usually the recipes didn't list such things because all good cooks of the 1800s knew the quirks of their own wood stove and how to bake in it. Rather than an oven temperature gauge, the woman stuck her hand in the oven and counted how many seconds she could stand the heat. This told her whether the oven was warm, moderate or hot. She also knew which type of wood burned in the stove worked best for which recipe.

Some recipes I expected to find, I didn't. These were very basic recipes that the cook kept in her head and didn't need to write down. Instead of precise measurements of cups or teaspoons, the ingredients were in pinches or handfuls. Some of these "mental recipes" were passed on to daughters, but many commented, "I could never make it taste quite like Mother's though."

My main goal in writing this book is to portray the everyday life of the women who homesteaded the prairie. By reading the quotes and recipes, I hope the reader appreciates the hard work the pioneer mother did for her family, and remembers their own past fondly.

Recipes from *Butter in the Well*

Go back to a time when there are no streets, roads or cars. Imagine there are no buildings, homes, hospitals or grocery stores around the corner. All of your family's belongings fit in a small wooden wagon. The year is 1868. There is nothing but tall, green waving grass as far as the eye can see. The scent of warm spring air after a morning rain surrounds you. Spring blows gently in your face. The snort of the horse and an occasional

Kajsa Svensson Runeberg

meadowlark, whistling its call, are the only sounds. You are alone on the virgin land of the vast prairie.

From the Introduction of **Butter in the Well**

March 31, 1868

By the creek on our land—*When we arrived in Salina today, we bought a wagon, an ox, a horse, lumber for the buildings, a 100-pound sack of flour and a few supplies. We spent practically all of our money in one day. . . .Carl picked out land east of the river on Section 30, Township 16 South, Range 2 West. It has a creek running through it and the river nearby. . . . The trees of the Smoky Hill River loom up within a half mile west of our homestead. No one lives in that area yet, so we will be free to hunt and fish along its banks. . . .*

Tonight and for quite a while we will sleep in the wagon and cook on the campfire. . . . Our basket of bread and salted meat that I packed in Ellsworth will last us awhile. I can see I'm going to have to be very creative in cooking this year until our first crops come in.

My mind today has been a constant jumble of questions. Will we survive by ourselves in the middle of nowhere?

Knäckebröd

2 cups milk	1 teaspoon salt
3 tablespoons butter	4 cups wheat flour
1/4 cup molasses	2 cups white flour

Heat milk. Add butter and molasses, then let cool. Stir in flour. Knead and roll out very thin. Prick with a fork. Bake in moderate oven until golden brown. Cut into pieces while warm.

Dried Beef

The round makes the best dried beef. For every 20 lbs. beef, use 1 pint salt, 1 teaspoon saltpeter, and 1/4 lb. sugar. Mix well together, divide into three parts, and rub well into the meat for three consecutive days. Keep the beef in a jar and turn it over frequently in the liquid which will form by itself. After it has soaked in this about a week, hang it up to dry, and after that smoke, if liked. When dry, sprinkle with pepper, tie up in paper bags, and hang up in a cool, dry place.

May 8, 1868
I'm getting good at cooking over a campfire, but I miss my oven for baking bread. We're eating a lot of beans, corn mush and biscuits that I make in the skillet. There is plenty of wild game in the area.

Baked Possum

———◆►◄◆———

Skin and clean possum, wash in cold water, salt in and outside, and let hang overnight. In the morning wash again and put in a baking pan with a little water. Cover and put it over the fire. When tender, remove top cover, baste meat with lard and dust with pepper. While meat is browning, peel potatoes, cut them in thick slices, and put them in a skillet over the fire with salt and a little water and lard. Cover, and let steam until tender. By that time the possum will be brown. Turn the potatoes over the possum and cook until potatoes are nicely brown.

Baked Coon

———◆►◄◆———

Skin the coon carefully, then remove the layer of fat, which is often an inch thick, right under the skin. This fat would give the meat a disagreeable, oily taste, if left on, but it nice and white, and can be used the same as leaf lard or for soap. Thoroughly wash the dressed coon in cold water and soak overnight in cold water with 1 tablespoon salt added to each gallon water. Bake. If the coon is old, as shown by large size, dark meat, and stiff hard bones and joints, it should be parboiled for 1 to 2 hours before roasting.

May 11, 1868
This morning we drove our wagon to the Robinsons' to get
the plow. . . . Fresh milk from their cow was a real treat for
all of us today. . . . Adelaide promised me a setting hen and
some eggs later in the spring when we have a place for them.

Cottage Cheese

———◆>◆<◆———

When whey begins to separate from clabber, it is ripe
to make cottage cheese. Stir thoroughly. Add the same
amount of boiling water as thick milk and set aside. When
cold, strain through a cloth and season to taste. A teaspoon
of baking powder greatly improves the flavor.

Deviled Eggs

———◆>◆<◆———

Boil hard as many eggs as desired, peel and cut length-
wise. Remove yolks and mince with salt, pepper, mustard,
vinegar, melted butter and a little sugar to suit taste. Refill
whites with the mixture.

Pickled Eggs

———◆>◆<◆———

Remove the shells from 3 to 4 dozen hard boiled eggs.
Carefully arrange in jars. Boil 1 pint vinegar with allspice,
ginger and a couple of cloves of garlic. Add another pint of
vinegar, bring to a boil again. Pour scalding hot mixture over
eggs. When cold, seal up jars for a month before using eggs.

May 11, 1868
*Adelaide gave me a loaf of rye bread, still warm from the
oven, to take home with us. We ate half of it before we got
back to the dugout.*

Rye Bread

4 cups water   2 cups rye flour
1/2 to 2/3 cup molasses   1 yeast cake
1 tablespoon lard   salt

Heat 2 of the cups water to a boil and pour over
molasses and lard. Add rye flour and stir until smooth, then
add salt. Add the rest of the cool water to make the batter
lukewarm, then add the yeast mixture and beat good. Work
in sufficient white flour to make into a very stiff dough.
Mold into four loaves and let raise again. Bake in a hot oven
for 10 minutes, then 35-40 minutes at a lower heat.

Oatmeal Bread

Scald 1 cup oatmeal with 1 pint boiling water and let
stand 1 hour. Add 1/2 cup of molasses, 1 teaspoon salt
(scant), 1/2 yeast cake dissolved in 1/3 cup of lukewarm
water. Add 1 quart of flour, let rise, shape in loaves, raise
again and bake in a quick oven.

May 15, 1868
I showed Adelaide the rashes on our arms, telling her that they itch so bad. She says it's the "Kansas Itch" that newcomers get and there's not much we can do about it.

Cooked Salve

2 1/2 lb. taly (sheep tallow)
1 lb. smör (unsalted butter)
1 lb. bivasc (bee's wax)
1 lb. harts (resin)
1/2 pint torpentine (turpentine)
Kamfort (camphor)
1 quart linolja (linseed oil)
1 pint alkohol (alcohol)

Swedish recipe for scrapes and sores. Mix together and smear on affected body parts.

Preventing Chapped Hands—When through with the work (especially cleaning, washing dishes and laundering), wash hands in vinegar, using 1 tablespoon of vinegar to one quart of water. Then rub the hands with mutton tallow, which has a healing effect. Hands should be dried thoroughly after each dabble in water, especially after washing clothes and going out in the cold to hang them.

Salve for itch—Mix sulphur and lard and grease up skin. After three days, wash with soap and grease again.

June 29, 1868

Went down to the river and picked mulberries early this morning. . . . I don't know what was more stained from the purple juice, my hands, the apron that I gathered them in, or Christina's face after she ate so many. I'm going to make a mulberry pie and dry the rest of the fruit for winter.

Mulberry Pie

Line a pie tin with crust, fill with fresh mulberries and 1 cup of sugar and bake open. When done, pour whipped cream over it.

July 1, 1868

I've gotten used to the heat, but today I swear it was over 100 degrees. I picked three bushels of wild plums from the thicket on the creek. Christina sat in the wagon jabbering to the ox. The bees and flies buzzed around my head as I pushed through the thicket. I scratched up my face in the process and tore a hole in my dress sleeve. Some of the plums had worms in them, but I'll dry them anyway.

To Dry Fruit

Slice fruit in thin slices and arrange in single layer on wooden tray. Cover with muslin and place trays in sun to dry fruit. After thoroughly dry, put dried fruit in containers with tight-fitting lids and store in a cool, dry, dark place.

July 29, 1868

I've been pulling weeds from our own cornfield and the garden. Killed five snakes today. They were seeking shade in my squash vines. We have been living on fresh tomatoes and corn. It feels so good to sink my teeth in a red ripe tomato and let the juice run down my chin!

Corn Fritters

1 jar of canned corn
4 well beaten eggs
2 tablespoons flour

2 tablespoons milk
salt and pepper to taste

Mix ingredients and fry in hot butter.

———

August 7, 1868

Since it was a calm morning, I made biscuits. It is too dangerous to start a campfire when it is windy. I made enough to last us several days . . .

Soda Biscuits

Mix 1 teaspoon salt, 1 teaspoon soda, 2 cups buttermilk, lard twice the size of an egg and enough flour to make a smooth dough. Bake in a hot oven.

September 28, 1868

First frost on the garden this morning. The vines were covered with a blanket of furry ice crystals at first sunlight, and by afternoon they were black and limp. Luckily I picked all the tomatoes last night, red and green, guessing that time was running out on the warm weather. . . . We have to use everything we harvest and make it stretch until next year.

Fried Tomatoes

———◆>◆<◆———

Peel red or green tomatoes and cut cross-wise in half-inch slices. Dip in beaten egg and sprinkle with salt, pepper and a very little sugar. Next dip in flour and fry in hot butter.

Green Tomato Pickles

———◆>◆<◆———

Slice 1 peck of green tomatoes. Sprinkle with 1/2 cup salt, let stand overnight and wash next morning in clear water. Heat 1/2 gallon cider vinegar, then add tomatoes, whole cloves, cinnamon and 1 cup sugar. Cook until clear and seal in jars.

Homemade Vinegar

———◆>◆<◆———

Mix 1 gallon warm water, 2 cups sugar and a yeast cake. Pour into a crock and add red apple peelings. Vinegar will be ready to use in 2 weeks.

September 28, 1868
I harvested the pumpkins and squash today, stacked some in the corner of the dugout and put the rest in the storage pit. I think we had a good first crop on the native prairie.

Canning Pumpkin

Pare and cut pumpkin in small pieces. Rinse in cold water and put in iron kettle without any extra water. Cover kettle and cook over slow fire for about an hour or until tender. For each large pumpkin used, add 1 tablespoon salt and 2 tablespoons sugar. Cook 2 hours longer, stirring often, then fill jars and seal at once. Keep in cool cellar.

September 28, 1868
I plan to harvest the beans tomorrow. . . . The easiest way to shell the beans will be to put the pods in the gunny sack, stomp on the sack to crush them, then pour them into the wash tub. The wind will blow the broken pod pieces away and let the beans fall into the tub.

Baked Beans

Soak 1 1/2 pints of beans overnight. In the morning, parboil in salted water. Put in bean pot with 1/2 lb. salt pork on top and 2 tablespoons each of brown sugar and molasses. Add just enough hot water to cover beans. Bake all day in moderate oven.

November 26, 1868
We celebrated the American holiday call Thanksgiving with the Robinsons today. . . . Benjamin had shot a turkey down near their bend of the river. . . . Adelaide also fixed venison, potatoes, creamed hominy corn, pickled beets, fresh wheat bread (I had two thick slices) and dried currant pie.

Fried Venison

Cut venison into medium thick slices, hack it criss-cross with a butcher's knife on both sides, roll in flour, sprinkle with salt and pepper, and fry in hot drippings until evenly browned on both sides. Take steak out of pan and put on a warm platter. Mix 1/2 cup milk and cream to the gravy in the frying pan and a very little flour to thicken slightly. Let boil up once and then pour over the steak, and serve at once.

Corn Pudding

1 jar cream-style corn
2 beaten eggs
2 tablespoons sugar
1 teaspoon salt
1/8 teaspoon pepper
1 1/2 cups milk
1 1/2 cups cracker crumbs
2 tablespoons melted butter

Mix first five ingredients and stir, then add milk. Pour into greased 1 1/2 quart dish. Top with cracker crumbs and butter. Bake for 1 hour.

Pickled Beets

beets
1 cup vinegar
1/2 cup water

1/2 cup sugar
1/4 teaspoon salt

Cook beets. After they are cool, peel and slice and put in jars. Heat other ingredients and pour over beets.

Brown Bread

1/2 cup sugar
1/2 cup molasses
2 cups sour cream or milk
1 teaspoon salt
1 cup white flour

2 1/2 cups graham flour
1 tablespoon melted butter
1 teaspoon soda dissolved
in hot water

Beat well and bake in loaves in moderate oven.

Currant Pie

1 cup currants
2 egg yolks

1 tablespoon flour
1/2 cup water

Bake in pie crust. Use egg whites for meringue.

December 25, 1868

She said "Merry Christmas" and I answered back "God Jul.". . . Adelaide gave me a mold of butter and a pan of ostkaka. Carl told her last week about how I had been craving it, so she attempted to make it for me.

They stayed for dinner. I served squirrel stew, potatoes, stewed pumpkin, biscuits, butter and wild plum jam.

Ostkaka

8 cups milk, warmed	3/4 cake rennet tablet,
3/4 cup flour	dissolved in a few drops
3/4 cup sugar	of water
2 eggs	little salt

Beat flour, sugar and eggs into a paste using 1 cup of the milk. Warm the 7 cups milk. (Test it on wrist like for baby's bottle.) Pour warm milk into buttered baking dish. Add rennet to warm milk, stirring slowly. Add egg mixture right away and keep stirring slowly until it starts to set or thicken. (Too much stirring will make it separate.) Bake in moderate oven, until brown and well set. Takes at least an hour.

Plum Butter

For each half gallon of wild plums, add 1 teaspoon soda to take out the bitter taste. Bring fruit to a boil, then pour off water. Put through a colander and for every 3 cups of pulp, mix in 2 cups of sugar. Cook until thick. Can and seal.

May 17, 1869

We have been eating lettuce, peas and new onions. The potato plants are blossoming and the corn is up.

Wilted Lettuce

salt to taste
3 tablespoons hot
bacon fat
1 egg
6 tablespoons vinegar

1 cup hot water
3 tablespoons sugar
Leaf lettuce,
chopped slightly

Cook ingredients but lettuce until it begins to thicken. Pour over lettuce and serve at once.

August 4, 1869

I also cut fresh corn off the cob and dried the kernels. Dried corn cooked in cream will hit the spot on a cold day this winter.

Dried Corn

Cook sweet corn on the cob in salted water for about 20 minutes. Cut from the cob, spread on shallow plates, and dry very slowly in a rather cool oven. Put the dried corn in sacks and place in a warm dry place. When wanted for use, soak 1 pint dried corn in cold water overnight, and if wanted for dinner, put over the fire about ten o'clock with a small piece of lean fresh pork or salt pork, 1 dozen potatoes, peeled and cut in small pieces, and water enough to cook.

October 12, 1869
The boys dug a root cellar east of the dugout to store our potatoes, root and vine crops. Andrew calls it 'the cave,' since it is so deep.

Storing Potatoes

———➤◄———

After digging the crop of potatoes, let cure outside for 2 to 3 weeks in a cool, shady place. When storing in the cellar, place a few apples in the potato pile. As the apples mellow, they will give off a fume that will keep the potato eyes from sprouting.

———

October 27, 1869
It is so good to have a milk cow at last! . . . I made cheese today. It was our custom at home to give the pastor a wheel of cheese for Christmas.

Cheese

———➤◄———

Pour 8 gallons of raw milk into a wash boiler and heat until lukewarm. Stir in salt and rennet softened in water, and stir slowly until curds form.

Pour the mixture into a large colander, lined with cheese cloth, and press the curd into a big round flat ball. When all the whey is pressed out, let set for 2 weeks.

November 12, 1869
We butchered two of the hogs today, and we had fresh pork
and gravy for supper. . . . Part of the meat has been salted
to be preserved and we are smoking the hams.

Liver Roast

Cover a fresh liver with boiling water for five minutes.
Drain. In bottom of baking dish, put 2 sliced onions, 2 sliced
carrots, 2 cups thick canned tomatoes, salt, pepper and a
generous sprinkle of flour. Dredge liver with flour and place
on top. Over this, place thin slices of bacon. Cover and bake
two hours. Add cut potatoes after first hour.

Smoked Barrel
for Bacon and Hams

Put a few live coals in an iron kettle, cover with clean
corn cobs, turn a clean barrel over this kettle, and smoke 2
hours at a time for 2 days. If smoked too long at a time, it
will shrink the barrel. When thoroughly smoked, put a brine
in the barrel made of 10 lbs. salt, 8 ounces saltpeter and 2
1/2 quarts molasses, for every 100 lbs. of meat. Add water
enough to cover the meat. Pack the meat in this brine and
weight down. The smoked barrel will impart the smoked
flavor to the meat.

Palt

When butchering the pig, catch the blood into a pan, and while still warm, whip blood to a pudding-like texture. Pour into 5 inch by 8 inch sacks made from a cotton flour sack, and cook. When ready to use, slice palt, brown in skillet and add milk. Stir to be a thin gravy.

Sylta

Clean hog's head of bristles, ears, eyes and inner ears. Saw head in pieces and cook until done. Remove the meat and grind up. Recook, seasoning with salt, pepper and allspice, then press into a bowl. Slice for table use. Some people prefer a few drops of vinegar on it.

Biggert

Cook hog's liver and grind. (Kidneys may also be cooked with liver and ground.) Cook meat off of hog's head and grind. For half hog's head, use about 1 lb. liver and about 2 cups oatmeal. Cook all 3 together on low heat and season to taste with salt, pepper, allspice, cloves and cinnamon. Store where cool.

When using, place 3 to 4 tablespoons of this in skillet and add as much milk as desired (about 1 quart.) When hot, thicken with flour and milk paste.

Pour over slices of bread to eat.

To Try out Lard or Suet

The soft fat should be cut in very small pieces and put in a kettle with a little water, and set over the fire to try out. While the lard is trying out, stir it up often with a long handled spoon or skimmer, and be very careful that it does not burn or scorch. When the little pieces of lard have shrunk to very small dark brown scraps, strain lard through a fine wire sieve into a perfectly dry and clean tin pail. When cold, cover the pail well and store in a cool, dry place.

Suet is tried out the same way. After the suet is tried out, pour in into a pan of ice cold water, and when hard, wipe it dry, wrap in white paper, and then put it in a linen or closed cloth bag and hang in a cool, dry place. Excellent for pie crust.

Canned Suet

Trim and chop suet fine, add salt to taste, and 1 cup molasses for every cup suet. Can in air-tight jars. This is fine to put in cakes or puddings and no other shortening will be needed.

To Keep Beefsteak

Fry beefsteak well done, then pack closely in jars and cover well with melted lard. Store in a cool place.

Brine for Pork

———◆►◄◆———

For 100 lbs. pork, allow 10 lbs. salt, 3 lbs. brown sugar, 2 ounces saltpeter, 1 ounce cayenne pepper and 4 1/2 to 5 gallons water. Let boil 5 minutes, skim well, let get perfectly cold, and then pour over meat packed in large jars or barrels. Put in a weight to keep the meat under the brine, cover the jar and set away in a cool place. Meat kept in this way is never rancid and flies do not get at it. In the spring, draw off the brine, boil it again, skim well, let get cold, and pour over the meat again.

Suet Pudding

———◆►◄◆———

2 cups chopped bread
1/2 cup chopped suet
1/2 cup molasses
1 egg
1 cup raisins

1 cup sweet milk
1/2 teaspoon soda
1/2 teaspoon cinnamon
a pinch of salt

Mix together all ingredients. Pour into a large greased tin can. Fill can about 2/3 full or less. Cover with wax paper tied with a string. Place in a kettle of water 2-3 inches deep. Cover and boil 2 hours.

Suet Pudding Topping: Mix 1 cup sugar, 1 teaspoon flour and 2 cups hot water. Mix and boil until clear. Flavor it with nutmeg.

November 12, 1869
Fader and Moder were over to help make the potatiskorv.
Moder and I chopped potatoes, onions and meat into fine
pieces, then Fader stuffed the mixture into the cleaned pig
intestine. . . . This is one of the special meats we save for
our Christmas Eve smörgåsbord.

Johan Magnus and Anna Lisa Andersson

Potatiskorv

After butchering hog, empty small intestines and turn inside out. Carefully rub with salt and scrape clean. Soak in soda water until they are white and clear.

Grind together a third of each—ground raw potatoes, ground beef and ground pork. Add salt, pepper and allspice to taste. Stuff in intestines. Keep sausage submerged in a weak brine solution to keep the potatoes from turning dark until you use them. When ready to cook, boil in water 30 to 45 minutes. Then brown.

December 25, 1869
*This year we celebrated Christmas with all the trimmings
and traditions of our family. I'll admit we used a primitive
substitute for most of our Christmas dishes, but Moder
makes the best ostkaka and frukt soppa no matter where she
lives. Adelaide gave us some white sugar to make some
kringlor, the pastry Carl likes.*

Fruktsoppa

1 1/2 lbs. dried fruit	1/2 cup tapioca
2 1/2 quarts water	3/4 cup sugar
1 stick cinnamon	juice of 1/2 lemon

Soak dried fruit, such as apples, apricots, peaches,
pears, prunes and raisins, overnight in water. Next morning,
add cinnamon and tapioca to fruit and simmer for an hour.
Add sugar and lemon juice and simmer another half hour.
Serve hot or cold.

Kringlor

5 cups lukewarm water	1 teaspoon salt
1 yeast cake	3 egg whites, beaten stiff
1/2 cup butter	little cardamon seed
1 teaspoon lard	flour

Make stiff with flour, let rise twice its size, roll out and
let rise again. Brush top with egg yolk-water mixture and
sprinkle with sugar. Bake.

December 25, 1869
I pickled catfish we caught in the river this fall and mixed it with potatoes and beets for Fader's favorite dish of sillsallad. It doesn't quite taste the same since it is supposed to be made with herring, but he was happy.

Sillsallad

1 small roast beef (no fat), cooked and ground
1 pickled or salted herring (skin and bones taken out)
1 apple, ground

3/4 cup cooked, cooled and chopped potatoes
1 qt. cooked beets, ground
1 onion, ground

Mix together and salt to taste. Add 1 tablespoon vinegar and mix. Chop up a boiled egg, white and yolk separately. Decorate salad alternately with eggs and beets. Just before decorating and serving, a little cream may be added to salad.

Pickled Herring

Soak 3 salt herring overnight in cold water. Clean, split and remove all bones and skin. Cut into small strips.

Mix 1 pint vinegar, 1 1/2 cups sugar and 2 teaspoons whole allspice together and bring to a boil.

Layer herring pieces and 2 sliced onions in a crock and pour cooled vinegar mixture over it. Let stand at least two days before using.

March 3, 1870
Christina has a cold this week. I made a mustard plaster.
When one of the children get sick I worry so. I wish there
was a doctor in our area.

Mustard Plaster

—•>+<•—

Mix 3 heaping tablespoons of mustard, 3 tablespoons flour and sufficient lard to form a paste. Spread this on old muslin and cover the mixture with two thicknesses of muslin. Apply plaster to the afflicted part.

—

May 20, 1870
The weather is slowly warming up, and the garden and corn have sprouted. If I can keep the jackrabbits out of the garden, I will have a better stand. Last night they ate down a whole row of peas. I believe I'm ready for some rabbit stew.

Stewed Rabbit

—•>+<•—

Dress, clean and joint a couple of young rabbits. Dredge in some flour. Put in a stew pan with a slice of lean ham, cut in small pieces, 1 tablespoon butter, 1 or 2 spring onions and 1 quart fresh green peas. Pour in a little milk, and let come to a boil, then draw to the back of the stove and let stew slowly until rabbit and peas are tender. Just before serving, season with salt and a very little sugar.

March 21, 1870

Carl's family will be joining us soon. Svärfar and Svärmor will bring Emma, Emanuel, Johan and Elenora. . . . They will be crossing the ocean on the Cunard Line steamer to New York, then taking the train to Kansas.

I never thought we'd see Sven Magnus and Katarina Andersson come to America.

Sven Magnus and Katarina Andersson

August 22, 1870
We moved out of the cellar and into our house today!...
Next Carl will have to build some furniture to fill up our
house. I want a big table, with a bench on either side ... A
cupboard on the north wall. . . our bed will be in the
northeast end ... And we need a wardrobe or dresser ...

Kitchen Floor Paint

Put 2 ounces of stick glue in 1 quart rain water and stand on back of stove until glue is dissolved. When cool, mix with yellow ocher until it will spread nicely. (Makes a nice brown color.) Now paint the floor. Paint drys the same day it is put on. When the floor is dried, go over it with boiled oil freely. This will wear like iron and you won't have to paint oftener than once every 3 or 4 years. It is good for porch if you like the color, and it is a very cheap paint.

Sawdust Dough

Thoroughly mix 4 cups sawdust and 1 1/2 cups wallpaper paste, adding enough water to make dough the consistency of biscuit dough. Keep hands moist, if they become sticky.

Use to repair furniture cracks due to shrinkage. Fill and allow cracks to dry thoroughly. Sand smooth when dry, then paint or finish.

Also may be used to model items. Let dry for 4 days.

September 5, 1870

We have been so busy this summer, with the crops and garden, and building our house. Two years ago I was out on the prairie all by myself. Now my family or Carl's drop by for coffee or a visit almost every day.

Raised Doughnuts

1 cup milk
1 egg
3 1/2 teaspoons sugar
1 teaspoon salt

2 tablespoons lard
flour
1/2 yeast cake

Roll and cut out with doughnut cutter. Set to raise like bread. Fry and roll in sugar.

Sour Cream Cookies

2 cups sugar
1 cup lard
1 cup cream
2 eggs beaten

4 cups flour
1 teaspoon soda
1 teaspoon vanilla
salt

Mix ingredients and bake.

October 30, 1872

Today we made our years' supply of soap. I had been saving the fire ashes for the lye, and lard from my cooking all year. I hate this job and hate to have the children in the area when we make soap. Lye burns the skin, and the throat if it is inhaled. After the mixture boiled to the right consistency, we poured it into pans to cool and harden.

Soap

Put 5 gallons of soft water in a 20-gallon kettle, add 7 cans lye and heat with a good brisk fire until the lye is all dissolved. Then put in 4 bucketsful, or about 10 quarts of grease and boil slowly until all the pieces of meat disappear, then let stand until cool. Next morning cut it out, being careful to get the white, clean part separate from the brown settlings. Make another batch of soap using more lye and water with the brown settlings. This should be enough soap to last an ordinary family a year.

Burns and Scalds—Cover with cooking soda and lay wet cloth over it. You can also use whites of eggs and olive oil or linseed oil, plain or mixed with chalk or whiting.

Fire in One's Clothing—Don't run, especially down stairs or outdoors. Roll on ground or carpet, or wrap in woolen rug or blanket. Keep the head down so as not to inhale flames.

December 12, 1872
Adelaide and Laura visited today and brought us some
apples as an early Christmas gift. Benjamin had bought
several bushels this fall in Salina. She made the apples into
apple butter, or dried rings, but had kept the best for eating
this winter.

Fruit Butter

2 lbs. fruit pulp
3 tablespoons vinegar
or fruit jelly
3 cups sugar
2 tablespoons lemon juice

3 tablespoons grated
lemon rind
1 teaspoon cinnamon,
1/4 teaspoon cloves,
few grains ginger

Use fruit pulp left from jelly making or make fresh
sauce. Cook with other ingredients until smooth and thick.
Fill jelly glasses according to directions for jelly.

Sweet Apple Pickles

Pare, cut in halves and core 1 peck of sweet apples, and
cover these overnight with 1/2 gallon of sugar. Next morning set over fire, and add 1 teaspoon each of cinnamon and
cloves. Cook until apples are easily stuck with fork. Add 1
pint of good cider vinegar and boil 5 minutes, then seal in
jars while hot.

February 14, 1873
We have had a round of colds this winter. I have brewed
many cups of Moder's cold remedy. I boil together catnip,
horehound and onions, and attempt to sweeten it with honey.
It is bitter, but it helps soothe the throat and clear the nose.

Horehound Taffy

Steep a one inch square of pressed horehound in two
cups boiling water for 1 minute, then strain through a double
cheese cloth. Add 3 cups sugar and 1/2 teaspoon cream of
tartar and boil until it will brittle. Pour on a buttered plate
and before it hardens, mark with a knife into small squares.

Honey Drops

1 pint strained honey   1 tablespoon lemon juice
1 tablespoon butter   few grains salt
1/8 teaspoon soda

Heat honey to the boiling point, and then add other
ingredients. Continue boiling until a hard ball is formed in
cold water. Pour into buttered pan. When cold pull until
white and porous. Cut into small pieces.

March 3, 1873
The geese are flying north today, so spring is around the corner. We ran outside to scan the sky when we heard the honks of the first flock overhead.

Roast Goose

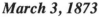

Dress and wash the goose thoroughly, and half fill with a dressing prepared as follows: Boil and chop fine 1 dozen onions and mix well with an equal quantity of bread crumbs. Add 1 teaspoon each of sage, salt and pepper. Bake in a hot oven, basting frequently. When done, skim off the fat from the gravy in the pan, add the liquid from the boiled giblets, and also the giblets chopped fine. Thicken with a little flour and season to taste. Serve goose with apple sauce.

A very nice dressing for goose is boiled sauerkraut, seasoned with pepper.

Boiled Duck

Boil duck with 1 large onion, 1 tablespoon vinegar, 1/2 teaspoon sage, and a little salt and pepper. When tender, remove the duck and boil down the liquor. Skim off the fat and thicken with a little flour browned in a pan with some butter. Return the duck to the gravy and let simmer a few minutes.

June 15, 1873
I let the milk sit in crocks in the cave for a few days to let
the cream rise to the top. Then I can skim it off and churn
the butter. I want to make extra butter and sell it at the
village by the grist mill.

Butter

Pour ripened cream into butter churn and churn for about 30 to 35 minutes until the butter is about the size of wheat grains. Draw off buttermilk and add cold water. Slowly churn for a few minutes, then draw off the water.

Put the butter in a wooden bowl and mix in 2 tablespoons of salt per pound of butter. Let stand a few minutes, then work butter with wooden paddle to get the last of the liquid out and the salt in. Press in crocks or butter molds and store in a cool place.

Butter and eggs ready for market

September 24, 1874
News of the grasshopper devastation and plight of the
people has spread throughout the nation. . . . We are living
on eggs and what little we had left in the cellars. The
chickens are the only animals that are well-fed because they
can feast on the thousands of dead grasshoppers still laying
around.

Angel Food Cake

Whites of 11 eggs	pinch of salt
1 1/2 cups sugar	1 teaspoon cream of tartar
1 cup cake flour	1 teaspoon vanilla

Sift sugar and flour together 7 times. Put cream of tartar
and salt in eggs and beat very light, fold in sugar and flour,
add vanilla. Put in cold oven and bake slowly 1 hour.

Make your own cake flour by sifting 4 cups flour and 1
cup cornstarch together four times.

Sunshine Cake

1 cup butter	11 egg yolks, beaten light
2 cups sugar	3 cups flour, sifted 3 times
1 cup sweet milk	with 2 tps. baking powder

Bake in tube pan 45 minutes. Use any flavoring desired.

February 26, 1875
Tonight neighbors came by foot, horseback and lumber wagon to the school dedication festival. . . . My kitchen was used to prepare the meal, since it is the closest house to the school.

Oyster Soup

Heat one quart milk, let come to a boil, add 1 pint oysters, 2 tablespoons butter, season with salt and pepper; boil two minutes and serve hot.

Lone Star School

September 29, 1875

We had so many pumpkins, we sliced and dried part of the crop to take up less room in the cellar. . . . My whole body sighed with relief when we got the garden harvested and stored for the winter. I have been worried all summer that something would happen and we would not have enough to eat. I'm not sure we could handle another winter like the last one.

Pumpkin Cookies

1 cup butter	1 teaspoon soda
1 cup sugar	1/4 teaspoon ginger
1 cup cooked pumpkin	1 teaspoon baking powder
a pinch of salt	2 cups flour
1 teaspoon vanilla	1/2 cup chopped nuts
1 teaspoon cinnamon	

Cream sugar and butter. Add pumpkin, salt, vanilla, cinnamon and ginger. Add soda and baking powder with flour and nuts. Drop by teaspoon on greased baking sheet, and bake in hot oven.

Green Pumpkin Pie

Cook yellow-green pumpkin until tender and rub through a colander. For each pint of pulp, add 3/4 cup sugar, 1 tablespoon each butter and flour, 3 tablespoons vinegar, 1 teaspoon cinnamon, 1 beaten egg and a little allspice. Bake between two pie crusts. Tastes similar to green apple pie.

September 18, 1876
We have been stripping sorghum this week. . . . The stalks are crushed and then the green juice is boiled down to dark brown molasses. . . . Sorghum molasses is so good on buttermilk pancakes.

Sweet Milk Pancakes

Beat 3 eggs, then add 2 cups milk. Add 2 cups flour, and 1 teaspoon each of salt and sugar. Add 2 cups milk. Bake on hot griddle. Makes a thin pancake.

Plättar

Beat 2 eggs, 2 cups milk and 1 cup flour until smooth, then add 2 tablespoons melted butter, 2 teaspoons sugar and 1/2 teaspoon salt.

Makes very thin pancakes that are good rolled up and served with fruit. Enough for two people.

Imitation Maple Syrup

Boil 1 dozen clean corn cobs (red are best), for 1 to 2 hours, in enough water to leave nearly 1 pint liquid, when done. Strain, add 2 lbs. brown sugar, and boil until as thick as desired.

December 22, 1876

I've had my hands full taking care of sick children. Alfred has recovered, but Willie still has a cough. Mr. Lapsley has been so worried about Willie that he brought over his favorite home remedy (turpentine and lard) to rub on Willie's chest.

Cough Syrup

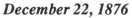

1/2 cup honey
2/3 tablespoon vinegar
1 tablespoon butter

dash of pepper
1/4 teaspoon powdered alum

Heat to boiling point. Take 1 teaspoon as needed for cough or hoarseness. May be taken cold, but is better and more effective used hot or warm.

For cough—Boil horehound candy and sugar or molasses to a tea stage and drink.

For croup, sore throat or tonsillitis—Mix the yolk of 1 egg, 1 tablespoon lard, 1 teaspoon each of camphor, turpentine and coal oil and 5 or 6 drops of carbolic acid. Thicken all with table salt, spread on the throat warm and cover with hot flannel.

For Pneumonia—Chop and heat 10 onions in skillet. Add the same amount of rye meal and enough vinegar to make a thick paste. Stir and let simmer 5-10 minutes. Put in a large cotton bag and lay on chest as hot as patient can bear. Continue applying hot packs every 10 minutes until perspiration starts freely.

May 13, 1877

Ola told that on that evening, the family was eating their Julafton smörgåsbord when a band of Indians broke into the house, intending to raid their meal. One Indian . . . thought the sauce had set his mouth on fire. . . . Unable to speak to the Indians in their words, Ola put just a dab of the mustard sauce on a piece of lutfisk and ate it to show the Indian that the sauce must be used sparingly. Ola's quick thinking spared the family. . .

Lutfisk

Soak dried fish sticks in rain water for 3 days. Pour off water and replace with fresh water, in which 2 tablespoons of sal soda and 1/2 cup lime has been added for each gallon of water needed to cover fish. Soak in this solution for 3 days then change water again. Soak for 3 more days, changing water each day. Boil to cook.

Hot Mustard Sauce

4 level teaspoons dry mustard
2 level teaspoons flour
1/4 teaspoon salt

Mix; then add enough cold water to make a thick paste. Gradually add boiling water, mixing well, to make a medium sauce with the right consistency. Mix well to avoid lumps. Use sparingly.

December 10, 1878

Peter. . . asked me to make a dish that his mother always makes for Christmas. . . . rispudding with kräm. He said it is made with rice, cream, eggs and sugar, but she adds ground cinnamon to it that makes it different. I started to say I was out of cinnamon when he reached into his coat pocket and pulled out a piece of cinnamon bark.

Rispudding

3 1/2 cups milk　　　　1/2 teaspoon salt
1/2 cup rice　　　　　　1/3 cup sugar
1/2 cup water　　　　　 1 teaspoon vanilla

Wash, then cook rice, water and salt until liquid is absorbed. Mix in milk and sugar; simmer until rice is tender, about 1 hour. Add vanilla. Cool and serve with lingonberries and cream, or kräm.

Kräm

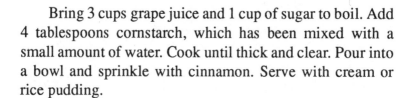

Bring 3 cups grape juice and 1 cup of sugar to boil. Add 4 tablespoons cornstarch, which has been mixed with a small amount of water. Cook until thick and clear. Pour into a bowl and sprinkle with cinnamon. Serve with cream or rice pudding.

November 21, 1879
*We have a problem with mice. . . . The tallow candles we
made yesterday have been chewed on. I left them lying on
the kitchen table last night.*

Tallow Candles

After fall butchering, melt tallow made from beef fat
and pour into candle molds which have a wick of braided
thread already in place in each mold. After tallow has
cooled, dip mold in warm water to loosen candles and they
will drop out when the mold is turned upside down. Wrap
and store in a cool place.

December 13, 1879
*We enjoyed the Lone Star School Christmas program this
evening. . . . Since there is such a large enrollment, the
schoolhouse was packed with family and friends. We ended
the evening with pie and coffee.*

Oh-So-Good Pie

4 eggs, (separate whites
and yolks)
2 cups sugar
3 tablespoons vinegar

3 tablespoons butter
1 cup raisins
1 teaspoon each—cloves,
cinnamon and allspice

Mix all ingredients together and add egg whites
(beaten) last. Bake in unbaked crust.

June 21, 1880

The threshing crew started on our wheat today. We have been busy making bread and pies to feed 12 extra people. This morning I started to pull the butter crock out of the well and the rope broke! . . . I hate to lose a crock like that, and there is just no way to retrieve the butter from the bottom of the well.

Sour Cream Pie

3 eggs
1 cup sugar
1 teaspoon cinnamon

1/2 teaspoon cloves
1 cup chopped raisins
1 cup sour cream

Beat egg yolks, add sugar, spices, raisins and cream. Fold in egg whites, beaten stiff. Pour into pastry shell. Bake in hot oven 15 minutes, then lower heat and bake until set.

Butterscotch Pie

1 teaspoon flour
1 cup brown sugar
2 egg yolks
1 cup milk

1/2 teaspoon vanilla
4 teaspoons butter
a pinch of salt

Combine sugar and flour in pan and heat. Add milk slowly, stirring until it thickens. Add slightly beaten egg yolks and cook 3 minutes longer. Remove from fire and add butter and vanilla. Pour into baked pie shell. Cover with meringue made of 2 egg whites. Brown in oven.

Lemon Chiffon Pie

———◦►◄◦———

3 egg yolks
3 tablespoons water

juice and rind of one lemon
1/2 cup sugar

Cook in double boiler until thick. Beat 3 egg whites and 1/2 cup sugar until stiff.

Lightly fold yellow part into the whites. Put in a baked crust and brown top quickly.

Raisin Lemon Pie

———◦►◄◦———

Boil 1 cup raisins and 2 cups water. Mix 1 cup sugar, 1 tablespoon flour and 2 eggs and add to raisins. Cook until thick. Add juice and rind of 1 lemon.

Lemon Pie

———◦►◄◦———

Make white sauce of 2 teaspoons butter, 2 teaspoons flour and 2 cups milk. Then add 1 cup sugar dissolved in the juice and grated rind of 1 lemon and boil. Add 2 egg yolks beaten light and boil a few minutes longer. Put in baked pie crust. Cover with meringue, use 1 heaping teaspoon sugar when beating meringue.

Add 1/4 teaspoon baking powder to egg whites when beating meringue for pie and it will never be tough.

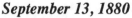

September 13, 1880
Anna and Ola had a daughter Lovinia Hildegard, today. I
went over to help her and fix meals for the family. Ola likes
my watermelon rind pickles, so I brought a small crock
along for him.

Watermelon Pickles

2 lbs. of watermelon rind
1 cup salt
4 quarts water
2 quarts vinegar
2 cups sugar
1/4 cup mixed pickle spices

Pare the rind and remove all the red portion of the
melon, cut it in strips or small squares and soak in salt water
overnight. In the morning, soak in fresh water for an hour
and drain. Tie the spices in a bag and put them in a saucepan
with the vinegar and sugar and boil about 10 to 15 minutes
until the liquid is clear. Add the watermelon rind and boil
until it is tender, but do not allow it to boil soft. Test it with
a straw. If the straw is easily inserted, take the rind from the
syrup with a skimmer and put it in glass jars. Boil the syrup
down a little longer until it gets somewhat thick and pour it
over the rind in the jars and seal airtight.

Never use tin, copper or brass vessels for pickling, as
the vinegar will eat into the metal and produce an unwhole-
some result.

September 28, 1880
The cellar is well-stocked this year. . . . We canned corn,
beans and beets. I have three crocks of cabbage in brine
down in the cellar. . . . It makes me feel good to see all of
the jars lined up on the shelves. So many shapes and sizes,
filled with hues of yellow, red and green.

Corn Salad

——➤◄——

24 ears of corn
2 heads of cabbage
8 good sized onions
2 tablespoons corn starch
5 cent package of
mustard seeds

2 cups sugar
4 green peppers
1/2 cup salt
1/2 gallon vinegar
2 tablespoons celery seeds

Cut corn off cob, dice vegetables and add other ingredients. Boil 10 minutes or more. Can up and seal.

Canned Bean Salad

——➤◄——

1 gallon green beans
2 cups vinegar
4 tablespoons butter
4 tablespoons sugar

4 tablespoons mustard
3 egg yolks, beaten light
onion to taste

Boil beans in salt water until tender. Add rest of ingredients, boil together and seal while hot.

Sauerkraut

————◦➤◄◦————

For a medium size wash tub of shredded cabbage, use about 3 or 4 handfuls of salt, 2 tablespoons caraway seed, 1 onion and 1 apple, chopped fine. Proceed in alternate layers until all the cabbage is used, pressing down each layer firmly, so that it will be under brine. Cover, let stand 2 days, then dip off all the old brine you can, and fill up with hot water. Cover and let ferment for 2 to 3 weeks. Each week check barrel, clean top stones, boards and cloth, and add hot water and salt if needed. Can be put up in jars when done, or left under brine in barrel.

Beet Relish

————◦➤◄◦————

1 quart of beets, boiled and chopped	2 cups sugar
	1 teaspoon pepper
1 quart of cabbage, chopped	1 tablespoon salt
	1 cup of horseradish

Add vinegar and boil till cabbage is done. Can up and seal.

Pickles can be colored nice and green by adding freshly gathered nasturtium leaves, horseradish leaves, grape or cherry leaves. But do not boil these with the pickle—just put a few of them in the top of the jar of pickles.

Cucumber Pickles

——→•←——

100 small cucumbers,   1 ounce cloves
each about 3 inches long   1 tablespoon salt
vinegar to cover   1 cup sugar
1 ounce mustard seed   2 red peppers, cut up

Put cucumbers in salt brine overnight, then scald with boiling water as many times as needed to freshen them. Dry with towel and when cold, place in kettle with vinegar to cover. Put spices in bags and add to pot. Scald slowly and when vinegar is boiling hot, they are ready to put away. In bottom of each jar, place a piece of alum the size of walnut and some horseradish root.

Dill Pickles

——→•←——

Wash cucumbers in cold water. Place a layer of dill in the bottom of keg. Fill the keg with cucumbers, ending with layer of dill on top. Close barrel and pour the following brine through bung hole; the proportion of 1 quart salt to 9 quarts water until barrel is filled. In 3 or 4 days, drain brine off and boil. When brine is cool, pour back into keg. Leave the bung hole open until the cucumbers begin to ferment, then close bung hole and let stand until ready for use. Be sure to keep cucumbers covered with brine at all times.

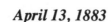

April 13, 1883
Erick was teasing Magdalena, . . . She turned beet red, explaining that the family in Smolan who she worked for were English, and of course she had some problems understanding them. She thought the mistress instructed her "to put the newly baked bread on the floor," so she did. The woman was talking about rolling the bread dough to be baked in flour, but the translation came out mixed.

White Bread

At noon, when the potatoes are cooked for dinner, select 3, each about the size of an egg and mash very fine. Add 1 tablespoon salt, 2 tablespoons sugar and 3 tablespoons flour. Mix well together, then add scant 3/4 cup boiling water, stirring vigorously, and when lukewarm, add 3/4 yeast cake dissolved in a little lukewarm water. Stir the mixture well, cover and let stand in a warm place. In the evening, scald 2 cups sweet milk, pour it into the mixing pan, add 2 cups cold water, and when lukewarm, add the light yeast mixture and mix stiff with warm flour. Turn out on the bread board and mold into a large loaf, kneading about 10 to 15 minutes. Return to the mixing bowl, cover and set in a warm place over night. In the morning, knead it down and divide into three loaves. Put into greased tins, and set in a warm place to rise until they have doubled in bulk. Bake one hour in a moderately hot oven.

December 25, 1884
It has been a happy, busy Christmas season. We baked dozens of cookies and breads. Each child has a favorite that we had to make. Besides what we wanted for company, we needed cookies for the children's school program, the neighbors' baskets and plenty to nibble on ourselves.

Kisslings

1 1/2 cups butter
3/4 cup sugar
1 cup ground almonds

4 cups flour
2 teaspoons vanilla

Cream butter and sugar. Stir in remaining ingredients. Roll out thin and cut in half-moon shapes. Bake, then roll in powdered sugar.

Peppernuts

2 cups butter
1 cup brown sugar
1 cup sugar
2 eggs
1 cup syrup

1 teaspoon each allspice,
cinnamon and nutmeg
1/2 teaspoon cloves
6 cups or more flour

Cream butter and sugar, then add eggs. Alternate dry ingredients and syrup. Stir in enough flour to make stiff dough. Roll out dough to make a roll the size of your finger and cut into bite size pieces. Bake.

White Sugar Cookies

1 cup butter	1 teaspoon soda
2 cups sugar	flavor
2 eggs	flour enough to roll
3/4 cup buttermilk	

Roll out dough, cut in shapes and bake.

Macaroons

Beat 3 egg whites until stiff. Add 1/4 teaspoon of cream of tarter and 1 cup sugar. Beat until very stiff. Drop by spoonfuls on baking sheet and bake in slow oven.

Moonshiners

4 egg yolks	4 tablespoons melted butter
4 tablespoons sugar	1/2 tablespoon vanilla
4 tablespoons cream	flour to roll out thin

Cut into diamond shapes and slit a hole in the center. Slip one corner thru the slit. Drop into hot fat and fry brown. Shake in sack with powdered sugar.

January 7, 1886
We have had a terrible blizzard the last two days. The drifts
are as high as the eaves on the south side of the barn. . . .
To keep the children occupied, we made a large batch of
skorpor. The smell of the milk-soaked bread, sprinkled with
cinnamon and sugar slowly drying in the oven lifted their
spirits.

Skorpor

2 cups sugar
1/2 cup butter
1 cup sour cream
1 cup nuts
1 egg

1/2 teaspoon soda
1 teaspoon baking powder
4-5 cups flour for
stiff dough

Mix and bake as a cake, then cut into strips and dry in
a slow oven until light brown.

Butter Fingers

1 cup butter
2 tablespoons sugar
2 cups flour

2 egg whites
1 cup chopped almonds
1/4 lb. crushed lump sugar

After mixing, roll dough into rolls the size of little
finger and 2 inches long. Dip is slightly beaten egg white
and roll in almonds and lump sugar. Bake in moderate oven.

March 7, 1886

Peter and Hannah bought the farm straight north of us. Peter missed farming, like I figured he would. He was over to see if we had any milk cows we would want to sell.

Peter and Hannah Olson and children

'Angel food
viten af 11 ägg ett och ett hälft glas
säker siktat ett glas mjöl siktat en half tesked
bakingpowder en half tesked Cream of tartar
blanda sakret och mjölet tillsamman och siktta
blanda bakingpowder och crimaftartar tillsamman
med sakret och mjölet och sikta det för dette
siktta till samman med äggviten en tesked venella
bakas i 40 minutar

Hannah Olson's Angel Food Cake Recipe

May 20, 1887
The rail crews and their teams of horses and mules have
camped in our south field while they are working on this
length of track. . . . I've made a little money by selling bread
and pies to the workers. . . . Julia has been handing out the
rolls one by one to the men.

Julia's Biscuits

2 cups warm liquid—
1/2 milk, 1/2 water
1 yeast cake
2 teaspoons salt

1/4 cup sugar
2 cups flour
2 tablespoons melted lard

Beat good. Keep adding flour (about 2 1/2 to 3 cups) and knead down. Form into pillows and let rise. Bake in a hot oven.

Graham Bread

3 cups lukewarm water
1/2 cup sugar
1 yeast cake
3 teaspoons salt

1/2 cup graham flour
2 tablespoons lard
about 6 1/2 cups flour

Mix and knead. Let rise until double. Punch down and let rise again. Form into loaves. Let rise. Bake in moderate oven.

December 31, 1888

Whenever I use a bowl or kitchen tool that Carl carved for me, I tell the girls stories about our early days. They can't imagine living in a dugout alone on the vast prairie. . . .
I have come to love my land in America. We worked hard to carve the fields out of the virgin prairie. Now I could not leave this patch of land in the middle of Kansas. This farm will always be home.

Kajsa Swenson, her children and Peter Runeberg

Recipes from *Prärieblomman*

To Alma,
For your sixteenth birth-
day, I am giving you a
blank book of pages. . . .
Years later this book will
bring back smiles and
tears to help you recall fa-
vorite places you never
meant to forget, cherish
lives lost, and to see how
yesterday's events become
tomorrow's history. . .
Keep this book with you
always. Your written
memories will sustain you
when you have moved on
to a prairie of your own
someday.
With love, Mamma

Alma Swenson

The Setting

Snow blankets the homestead on this quiet Sunday after-
noon in 1889. Silent white-iced furrows in the fields of the
159 acres wait for spring planting. . . .
The dirt road running by the farm was just a trail not too
many years back. Life and growth have progressed for the
family, but there are still patches of native grass beside the
homestead to remind them of their start on the prairie.
Peering into the parlor window facing south, you get a
glimpse of petite Alma Swenson. . .

From the Prologue of *Prärieblomman*

__January 28, 1889__
I was up to my elbows in hot sudsy water this morning scrubbing dirty shirt collars and skirt hems on the washboard. . . . Unless there's a blizzard or it's raining on Mondays, it's a weekly job that has to be done outside because we have to heat the large iron kettle of water over an open fire.

Laundry Hints

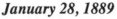

To remove axle grease or other grease from clothing, rub butter on spots before washing it.

To remove rust spots from fabrics—Moisten, rub on cream of tartar, and place in the sun.

To remove rust from colored fabric—Rub spot with raw onion and leave on an hour, then wash as usual, giving the spot a little extra rub.

Wet a fruit stain with camphor before washing and it will wash out easily.

To remove paint in flour sacks—Soak in soda water, then wash in soap water. Put in cold water and coal oil, and bring to boil.

To wash colored calicoes—Dissolve 10 cents worth of sugar of lead in six to eight quarts of rain water. After the garments are washed and rinsed, dip them in the mixture and ring out. It not only sets the color but keeps it.

To remove mud stains from fabrics—Rub with cut raw potato or sponge with weak ammonia or with baking soda dissolved in water.

When ironing starched clothes, put some kerosene on a cloth, and rub iron on it every time iron is taken from the stove.

Before hanging out clothes during winter, wipe the line with a cloth wrung out of vinegar. This way you can keep clothing from sticking to the clothesline.

Remove grease from garments by sponging with one tablespoonful of salt to four of alcohol.

Washing clothes

February 6, 1889

The kitchen table legs thumped the floor in rhythm this morning as Mamma kneaded and pounded the bread dough for the multitude of mouths we feed every meal. This is a ritual that has happened probably every Wednesday and Saturday of Mamma's entire adult life.

Mamma's Bread

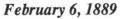

Mix together 2 quarts flour, 1 tablespoon sugar and 1 tablespoon salt.

Pour warm potato water over mixture and stir until thin dough. Add 1 1/4 yeast cakes dissolved in lukewarm water.

Let rise overnight. Add 1 quart lukewarm water, another 1 tablespoon salt, and flour to make thick dough. Let rise and knead and then let rise again. Put in pans and let rise, then bake one hour.

March 27, 1889

Little sister Mabel's first birthday. I made a sponge cake and Carrie whipped cream for topping for the celebration. Using both hands she dove into a carefully frosted creation, squeezing the topping between her chubby baby fingers.

Sponge Cake

Mix 1 cup powdered sugar, 4 eggs, 1 cup flour, 1/2 teaspoon baking powder and flavor to taste. Beat yolks and sugar until very light, beat whites to a stiff froth, and baking powder with flavor. Bake.

May 5, 1889
Mamma wrapped the last of the fried chicken and biscuits
in a cloth-lined basket to send home with Mr. Lapsley for
his meal tomorrow.

Sour Cream Biscuits

2 cups flour   1/2 teaspoon soda
1 cup sour cream   1/4 teaspoon salt
1 teaspoon baking powder

Sift salt and baking powder with flour. Stir the soda in
the cream. Mix all together. Handle lightly on a well floured
board. Bake.

Chicken Pie

Cook chicken until it falls from the bone and place it in
a baking dish.

Make a sauce of 3 tablespoons melted butter, 3 tablespoons flour, 5 cups broth and 1 cup milk. Pour over
chicken.

Over this spread a batter made of the following: 2 cups
flour, 2 teaspoons baking powder, 2 tablespoons lard, 1 egg,
1 cup milk and pinch of salt.

Bake to a golden brown.

June 15, 1889
Mamma's 45th birthday. Taking a break from our daily routine. . . we celebrated by attending the ice cream social at Hessler's grove in Assaria this evening.

Vanilla Ice Cream

4 eggs
2 1/2 cups sugar
6 cups milk

4 cups light cream
2 tablespoons vanilla
1/2 teaspoons salt

Beat eggs till light. Add sugar gradually, beating until mixture thickens. Add remaining ingredients. Mix and freeze.

Strawberry Ice Cream

1 pint berries
1 cup milk

1 cup sugar
1 tablespoon lemon juice

Crush berries. Add sugar, lemon juice and milk.
Partially freeze, then mix in 1 cup whipped cream and freeze again.

July 12, 1889
Kerr's threshing crew is here this week to thresh the wheat.
I have lost count of the number of pies and cakes I have
made.

Pie Crust

Mix together 3 cups flour, 1 cup lard and a 1 pinch salt, then add 1/2 cup cold water. Roll out for pies.

Grape Pie

1 1/2 cups grapes   1 tablespoon melted butter
2 cups sugar   2 well beaten eggs
pinch of salt

Separate pulp and skins, heat pulp and remove the seeds. Mix with other ingredients. Put between crusts and bake in a moderate oven.

Strawberry Pie

Beat whites of 2 eggs until stiff and dry. Add 1 cup sugar and stir thoroughly. Fold in 2 cups of strawberries, being careful not to break them. Pour into a pie shell that has been baked and cooled, and bake in a very moderate oven. A hot oven spoils the meringue, and too slow baking draws the juice from the berries.

August 29, 1889
Rows of jelly jars and canned fruit already line half the
shelves in the cellar from our work this summer. As the
nights grow cooler, the rest of the garden crops will be
plucked from the vine or uprooted from the earth.

Vegetable Soup

1 gallon potatoes
3/4 gallon, mixed of
carrots, parsnips,
tomatoes and cabbage
2 quart peas
12 onions
1 chicken

1 pint each of corn,
turnips and beans
1 quart each of cooked
 brown beans, celery
and asparagus
parsley to season
salt and pepper

Cut up and cook vegetables separately, then mix and can. Most any vegetable can be added or omitted. Makes 25 pints.

Canned Cucumbers

Wash in cold water and pack in jars. For each quart green cucumbers packed in glass jars, mix 3 tablespoons sugar, 2 tablespoons salt, 2 tablespoons mustard with white vinegar and pour over cucumbers. Add a pinch of alum on top of cucumbers and fill jar full with vinegar mixture. Seal. Turn jars up and down to mix the dressing.

December 13, 1889
After the coffee had cooked and I arranged a plate of rolls and cups, I started the Christmas season by waking the family up with St. Lucia's song and serving them coffee in bed. According to the medieval legend, St. Lucia, dressed in white with a crown of glowing candles encircling her head, fed the poor and hungry.

Cinnamon Rolls

1 cup sugar
1/2 cup butter
2 teaspoons salt
7 cups flour

2 yeast cakes
2 eggs
1 pint water

Dissolve yeast in 1/2 cup of the water. Add rest of the ingredients. Mix until stiff. Cover and let rise. Punch down and let rise again. Roll out for cinnamon rolls or coffee bread. Bake.

Egg Coffee

Bring water to a boil. Beat egg, including shell, until yolk and white are well mixed. Mix with ground coffee and a little water. (Use a teaspoon egg per cup of coffee.)

Stir into boiling water. Turn off heat and let stand until bubbling stops. Bring just to a boil again, turn off heat. Add 1/4 cup of cold water. Let stand about 10 minutes until coffee grounds have settled before serving.

January 18, 1890
. . . we trooped into the cold parlor last Sunday afternoon to dismantle the Christmas tree. . . . Mamma carefully wrapped her glass balls as we plundered the tree, eating all the edible ginger cookie ornaments we found hidden among the branches.

Ginger Cookies

1 cup sugar
1 cup lard
1/2 cup sorghum
2 eggs

3 teaspoons soda mixed in
1/4 cup hot water
2 teaspoons ginger
flour to roll

Roll out, cut out shapes and bake.

February 15, 1890
The Star Literary meeting had a valentine theme tonight. . . . . women brought special treats for refreshments. I baked and decorated a cake for my contribution.

Sour Cream Cake

1 1/2 cups sour cream
1 1/2 cups sugar
3 eggs, well beaten
2 1/2 cups flour
2/3 teaspoon soda

2 1/4 teaspoons
baking powder
flavoring—Chocolate or
 burnt sugar

Mix and bake.

April 25, 1890

Gentle sprinkles broke my concentration while I was beating the dirt out of the parlor rug, so I had to quit and lug it back inside. We're hitting spring cleaning with a vengeance. Yesterday we washed windows.

Household Cleaning

Furniture polish—Equal parts of sweet oil, vinegar and turpentine makes the best possible furniture polish. Apply with a cloth, rub well and shake often when using.

To keep spilled liquids from staining a rug, cover the spot immediately with salt. The salt will absorb the liquid.

To prevent dust from scattering when sweeping, put a little kerosene on broom until it is slightly oily. Pour oil around handle where bristles are attached and it will saturate broom.

A few drops of ammonia kneaded into a small amount of bread dough makes an efficient wall paper cleaner.

Clean rugs and overstuffed furniture with cornmeal or sawdust soaked in kerosene. Apply with brush. Air the object well after cleaning and beware of open flames.

Ammonia will make all glass shine if a small amount is used in the washing water.

To remove hard grease spots from a stove, put a few drops of kerosene oil on a cloth, and rub spots with it.

Sprinkle wheat flour on grease spots on carpet as soon as they happen. Sweep up every few days and apply more flour until spots are gone.

Cover fresh soot spots on carpet with salt before sweeping up to avoid a black stain.

Unslacked lime is excellent for cleaning small articles in steel, such as jewelry, buckles and the like.

A little quicklime placed in the infested places will drive away any kind of ants.

To remove rust from steel articles, rub with sweet oil, leave for twenty-four hours, then sprinkle with unslacked lime and rub off.

Household Repair

To cover furniture scratches—Unsalted nuts are preferable, but if you have only salted ones, remove the skin and break off a bit to expose the meat. Then proceed to rub the scratch with the grain of the wood. Brush away the nut crumbs as they form, with a soft cloth.

Crack filler—Make a paste of cornstarch and boiled linseed oil. Work this putty-like mixture into any crack with a knife and let it dry before varnishing or painting over it.

To remove varnish—Mix 1 quart cooked cornstarch and 2 tablespoons lye and rub on wood. Scrap off and wash with soap water and vinegar.

May 27, 1890
Light early summer breezes wafted through the Bridgeport
festivities for Decoration Day today. . . . savored the first
taste of this year's ice cream as we watched the Assaria
baseball team beat Bridgeport 25 to 5.

Cooked Ice Cream

For one gallon of ice cream, mix 1 quart milk, 4 egg yolks, 1 cup sugar with a heaping tablespoon of flour. Cook this until it thickens, then add the beaten egg whites and remove from the fire. Add another cup of sugar and 1 tablespoon of any flavor extract with 2 cups cream and enough milk to finish filling the gallon freezer within 3 to 4 inches from the top. Freeze.

Caramel Ice Cream

Put 3/4 lb. sugar in an iron skillet and brown a light brown. Add a little milk and cook slowly until the sugar is dissolved. Add 1 teaspoon cornstarch that has been dissolved in a little milk. When it boils, add 3 pints rich milk and another 3/4 lb. sugar and freeze. When partly frozen, add 1 pint cream which has been whipped and freeze hard. Chopped nuts may be added.

November 19, 1890
. . .we fried down the meat and packed it in crocks, sealing
the top with hot lard to keep the meat from spoiling.

Canning Meat, Poultry and Sausages

Cut the meat or poultry in pieces of convenient size, trim carefully, and be sure they are sweet and clean. Boil until tender in enough water to cover, seasoning to taste, and when all the meat is well done and tender, press a little at a time in hot glass fruit jars. Pour in a little of the hot gravy (which should first have been boiled down until it is almost ready to jelly when cold) into the jars, until the gravy fills up all the vacant places around the meat, but not enough to cause the meat to float. Then press in another layer of meat and more gravy, and proceed in this way until the jar is filled up to within one inch of the top. Be very sure that there are no air spaces left in the jars. Then fill each jar overflowing full with melted suet and seal air tight. Set the jars away in a permanent storage place, which should be cool, dark and dry and do not move the jars after once setting away. The melted suet on top will harden and moving the jars after the suet has hardened is apt to break the seal.

Sausages should be pricked and boiled in water until tender, and packed in jars the same as meat, with a layer of melted lard or suet on top. Everything should be boiling hot when canned, sealed air tight, and set away while hot.

November 19, 1890
After the hams are done soaking in brine water and smoked
for four weeks, they are hung in the cellar. When we need
to fix ham for a meal, we cut off a hunk and cook it.

Sugar Cured Meat

After butchering, cool the meat thoroughly and cut into family-sized chunks. Rub each chunk with coarse salt and set aside for 24 hours. Tightly pack the meat in an earthen vessel—a syrup barrel is good—putting hams and shoulders in the bottom and bacon slabs on top.

Heat 4 gallons of water. Let water boil and then cool a little before adding the following ingredients. For each 100 lbs. meat, weigh out 10 lbs. salt, 4 lbs. brown sugar and 2 ounces saltpeter. Let mixture cool thoroughly and pour over meat. This amount should be sufficient to cover the meat in the vessel.

Put on a wooden or china cover over the top and weigh it down with a stone to keep meat under the brine. If it isn't enough brine to cover the meat, add more. Put vessel in cool place and let stand for 6 weeks (ham) and only 1 week for the bacon slabs. If hams are large, leave in for 8 weeks. Take meat out of brine, then hang and smoke it.

To keep Meat without Smoking

After the animal heat has gone out of the meat, pack the pieces away in dry salt for 4 weeks. Then dip each piece in a very strong solution of boiling hot salt water. Dry off and rub thoroughly with borax and black pepper.

January 27, 1891
*For my 18th birthday I went back to school—for the day.
The pupils are studying the Civil War, so Mr. Lapsley held
the floor today. . . . I invited him over for a piece of birthday
cake after school. With Julia and Mabel's attention, he told
more stories between bites of cake and sips of coffee.*

Walnut Cake

1/3 cup butter	1 3/4 cups flour
1 cup sugar	1/2 teaspoon salt
3 egg yolks	1/2 cup milk
2 3/4 teaspoons	3/4 cup walnuts
baking powder	2 egg whites

Work butter until creamy; add 1/2 cup sugar, stirring
until light. Then add egg yolks, beaten until thick and lemon
colored. Measure flour, after sifting once, and sift two or
three times with the baking powder and salt. Then add
alternately to mixture with the milk. Add nut meats, broken
in pieces, and beat thoroughly. Beat egg whites until stiff
and gradually beat in remaining 1/2 cup sugar. Cut and fold
into first mixture. Put in a greased tube cake pan, bottom of
which has been lined with paper, bake 45 minutes in moderate oven. Remove from pan, cool and cover with Caramel
Frosting.

Caramel Frosting—Mix 1/2 cup boiling water with 1/2
cup burned sugar and 1 scant cup white sugar in a pan and
boil until it threads. Beat 1 egg white very stiff and gradually
beat in the boiled sugar. If it hardens too fast while beating,
add a little boiling water. When cool, it should be stiff.

May 15, 1891
After hand kneading enough dough for our needed supply
of bread, I was ready to spend the afternoon in the garden
while Mamma baked the dozen loaves in the hot kitchen.

Freshly baked loaves of bread

Everlasting Yeast

Boil 4 medium size potatoes and run through a fruit press. Add enough potato water to make 2/3 of a quart. Mix in 4 tablespoons of sugar. Set in a warm place until it ferments and bubbles form on top. Use 1 cup each time you bake. Replenish the yeast by adding potato water and sugar as needed. Store in a tight glass jar in a cool place.

Salt Rising Bread

3/4 cup sweet milk
4 tablespoons corn meal
1 tablespoon salt
1 tablespoon sugar

1 tablespoon lard
1 cup warm water
for each loaf
flour to make soft sponge

Scald milk, let cool a little, add corn meal, salt, sugar and lard. Put in warm place, 100 degrees for 8 to 10 hours. It should then be light and foamy. This is yeast and upon it depends the success of the bread. Next day, add 1 cup water for each loaf wanted and make sponge. Let rise to twice its bulk, then add more flour to knead quite soft. Make into loaves. Let rise again to double its bulk. Bake.

Salt rising bread should not be mixed as stiff as yeast bread.

Potato Rolls

---

1 cup flour
1 cup mashed potatoes
3/4 cup lard
1 cup sweet milk
2 eggs, well beaten

1/2 cup sugar (scant)
salt to taste
1/2 cup lukewarm water
1 yeast cake

Mix all ingredients, adding flour and yeast (mixed with water) last. Set to rise for two hours in a warm place, add 5 to 6 cups flour. Let rise again, mold into rolls, rise again and bake in moderate oven.

Crescent Rolls

1 yeast cake
1/2 cup sugar
1/2 cup butter
1 cup warm milk

salt
3 eggs beat light with sugar
4 cups flour, maybe more

Roll out and cut like pie pieces and roll. Let rise then bake.

Kaffebröd

3/4 cup milk
2 yeast cakes
1/2 cup lukewarm water
2/3 cup sugar
5 cups flour

1/2 cup butter
2 eggs
1 teaspoon salt
1 teaspoon powdered cardamom seed

Mix like for breads. Knead and punch down dough twice. Shape into buns or braids. Brush with melted butter and sprinkle with a mixture of sugar and cinnamon. Bake in a moderate oven for 15 minutes, then reduce heat to slow and continue baking for 15 more minutes.

Uncooked Butter Icing for Sweet Breads—Cream 1/2 cup butter and 2 cups powdered sugar. Add 1/2 teaspoon vanilla extract.

July 4, 1891
Spent the day harvesting wheat instead of celebrating Inde-
pendence Day. . . . Carrie's fresh squeezed lemonade and
my smörbakelser were greatly appreciated when we brought
refreshments out to the wheat field this afternoon.

Smörbakelser

Rub 1 egg yolk in with 1/2 cup sugar and 1 cup butter.
Add enough flour to make dough hard enough to thumb out.
Bake.

Oatmeal Cookies

1 cup butter
1 cup sugar
1 egg
1 teaspoon soda
2 1/2 cups flour

2 1/2 cups oatmeal
1/2 teaspoon salt
4 tablespoons sour milk
1 teaspoon vanilla

Cream butter and sugar, then add egg, then rest of
ingredients. Roll out as thin as possible. Cut in round shapes.
Bake on greased sheets in moderate oven for 8 - 10 minutes.

Egg Lemonade

Beat 1 egg with 1 tablespoon sugar. Add the juice of 1
lemon, fill the glass with cold water. Stir well.

July 4, 1891

Supper laid out on old quilts was eaten by the whole family in the field tonight. With daylight lasting until after nine, the men will work until dark. For a special treat for the holiday, I dug new potatoes to add to the creamed peas for supper.

Three teams plowing the field

Creamed Peas and Potatoes

Boil peas for 20 minutes, then add small potatoes. Put in 1 teaspoon salt, and boil 20 minutes longer. Pour off the water and add 1 cup cream and 1 teaspoon butter. Heat and serve.

Potato Salad

6 good sized potatoes,
  boiled and sliced
1 onion, minced
small cup of sour cream
2 tablespoons vinegar

2 tablespoons sugar
1/2 teaspoon salt
a generous dash of pepper
2 hard boiled eggs,
  chopped

Be sure that the potatoes are real cold after boiling before slicing.

Pressed Chicken

Cook young chicken until chicken is tender enough to fall from bones. Take out of cooking water and when meat is cold, put through coarse part of the meat chopper. Season to taste. Boil broth down to a pint and mix in with the chicken. Place in a mold and chill.

Corn Bread

Beat together 2 eggs and 2 cups of sweet milk. Then mix 2 cups of corn meal, 2 cups flour, 1/2 cup sugar, 1/2 teaspoon salt, 3 teaspoons baking powder, mix all together. Lastly stir in 1/2 cup butter melted. Bake in a quick oven.

Currant Cake

————— ✦ —————

1 cup sugar
1/2 cup butter
1 egg
1 1/2 cups sour milk
1 teaspoon soda

1 cup currants,
rolled in a little flour
1/2 teaspoon cinnamon
1/2 teaspoon cloves
2 1/2 cups flour

Mix and bake in hot oven.

Never-Fail Jelly Roll

————— ✦ —————

1 cup flour,
sifted before measuring
1 teaspoon baking powder
1/4 teaspoon salt

4 eggs, separated
1 cup sugar
1 tablespoon cold water
1 teaspoon vanilla

Sift flour, baking powder and salt 2 times. Beat egg yolks to lemon color. Beat egg whites until stiff and add to yolks. Add water, and sugar gradually and vanilla. Fold in flour and pour into buttered and floured 15 x 10 inch pan. Start in slow oven until raised, then increase heat 12-15 minutes. Loosen sides, turn upside down on damp towel sprinkled with powered sugar. Roll in towel and when cool, remove and spread with jelly. Roll up again and serve in 1 inch slices.

August 24, 1891

I spied a tramp walking toward the house from the railroad tracks. . . . I refilled the well bucket and offered the man the tin cup that always hangs on a hook on the well's windlass. . . . Mamma won't let tramps in the house, but she made two big sandwiches for him to eat while he sat under the front shade tree to rest.

Getting a drink of water from the well

Dried Beef Sandwich

Pour cold water over 1 glass of dried beef, then drain. Run through a grinder. Mix with 2 tablespoons mustard and a 1/3 cup sweet cream. Spread on slices of bread.

Egg Sandwich

Chop hard boiled eggs until they form a paste, add a little flavoring and mix the whole with mayonnaise dressing. Spread on slices of bread.

Ham Sandwich

Mince ham and hard boiled eggs. Mix with mayonnaise and spread between slices of bread. Add a leaf of lettuce between slices, if available.

Mayonnaise Dressing

Yolks of 3 eggs
1 teaspoon mustard
1 tablespoon sugar

3 tablespoons melted butter
sprinkling of pepper and salt
1/2 cup warm vinegar

Mix first six ingredients, then add to vinegar. Boil a few minutes until thick as custard.

June 16, 1892
If I'm not in the middle of a cherry tree picking fruit this week, I'm pitting the seeds, or sweating over the stove canning the dozens of jar of cherries we'll put up for the winter.

Cherry Preserves

After cherries are pitted, cover them with vinegar and let stand overnight. Drain and add a cup of sugar for each cup of fruit. Set aside and stir every day for seven days or until sugar is entirely dissolved. Put in jars and seal without cooking.

June 16, 1892
Mamma made several cherry pies today and us girls walked down to Mr. Lapsley's this evening with one for him. We spent a blissful hour sitting on his porch steps, listening to his tales while he savored a piece of the juicy fresh pie.

One Crust Cherry Pie

1 pint cherries, heated	2 tablespoons flour
1 cup sugar	3 egg whites

Bake a pie shell. While cherries are hot, mix in sugar and flour. Pour into crust. Whip egg whites and 3 tablespoons sugar until stiff. Brown in oven.

August 26, 1892

Christina is here this week helping with the apple harvest. Several bushels are sliced and layered on cheese cloth-covered screens to dry into shriveled leather rings of dried fruit for fruktsoppa and pies. All day a pot of diced apples slowly simmers for apple butter.

The light yellow tint starting to show on the green pears means the last crop from the orchard will soon be ready. Cherries were picked in June and the peaches and apricots in July. Instead of plum trees planted in the orchard, we raid the wild plum thicket along the creek.

Sulphured Apples

Peel and fill a market basket two-thirds full of apples quartered and the quarters cut into about three pieces. The apples must be free from all bruises and other blemishes.

In the bottom of a large barrel, place a pot of red coals. Sprinkle 3 tablespoons of sulphur on the coals. Hang the basket of apples by its handle on a rod laying across the top of the barrel, being sure the basket does not touch the coals. Cover the barrel top with an old piece of carpet and let smoke 45 minutes. When smoked, store apples in crocks or jars.

When ready to use, wash the apples good or put on the stove with some water and bring to a boil and pour the water off. They taste like fresh apples. Can be used for pies or sauce.

Scum on Jellies and Jams—Add a teaspoon of butter to mixture after it has come to a boil. This eliminates skimming off the foam and also improves the flavor.

Apple Jelly

Wipe apples. Remove stem and blossom ends and cut in quarters. Put in preserving kettle and add cold water to come nearly to top of apples. Cover and cook slowly until apples are soft. Mash and drain through coarse sieve. Avoid squeezing apple pulp through sieve. Allow juice to drip through a double thickness of cheese cloth. Boil juice 20 minutes and add 3/4 quantity of sugar; boil 5 minutes, skim and turn in glasses. Let stand 24 hours. Cover and keep in cool dry place.

Three-in-One

1 quart each of plum, peach and pear pulp
3 quarts sugar

2 teaspoons cinnamon
1 teaspoon ground cloves
ginger or allspice, if desired

Cook until thick. Seal in jars.

Canning Plums

Wash fresh firm fruit. Prick each plum in several places to prevent skin from bursting. Pack in hot, scalded jars. Fill to within an inch of the top with a boiling hot syrup of 1 part sugar to 1 part water. Seal and store in cool dry place.

November 14, 1892

We spent the day at Aunt Magda's to help butcher and preserve their winter supply of meat. After the cold weather prohibits the meat from spoiling, we move around to each family's house. With several people doing assigned tasks, the job goes much easier.

Magdalena and Nels Johnson and family - 1899

Scrapple

Boil 1 hog's head until tender. Remove from bone. Grind meat and return to broth. Grind 1 liver which has been boiled and add to broth. When boiling, add salt, pepper and 1/2 gallon corn meal, or enough to harden when cool. Slice and fry.

Smoked Pig Paunch

Thoroughly clean a pig paunch, or stomach, and boil until done. Chop and cook enough lean pork that it will require to fill the stomach and mix with it a 1/2 teaspoon saltpeter, salt, pepper and cloves. Pack into stomach securely, sew up and then return to the liquor in which the stomach was boiled. Let boil slowly 1 hour. Remove from fire and let remain in this liquid overnight. Then drain and smoke 6 days. Hang in a cool, dark, airy place. When wanted, cut in thin slices and serve without cooking.

Pickled Pig's Feet

Remove the toes and scrap clean. Soak the feet overnight in cold water. Next day boil until very tender, and salt before they are done. Pack in a stone jar and cover with hot, spiced vinegar, using whole cloves, allspice and pepper. Can be served as is, or heated up in boiling water. It is also good when split, rolled in flour and fried in hot fat.

Pickled Tongue

For the brine, allow 1 gallon water, 3 lbs. salt, 4 ounces sugar and 2 ounces saltpeter. Boil and cool, then put in the trimmed and cleaned tongues in crocks, and weight to keep them under the brine. When ready to use a tongue, soak overnight in cold water, boil until tender, skim, remove skin, slice and serve with mustard.

Fried or Scrambled Brains

Soak the brain in salt water overnight, then remove the thin skin.

For fried brains, slice once, roll in flour and fry brown on both sides in hot lard or butter.

For scrambled brains, heat 1 tablespoon butter in a skillet and when hot, put in the brains, stirring constantly, until almost dry. Then add 2 beaten eggs and stir until firm. Add salt to taste.

Preserving Meat Joints

For each joint, allow 2 tablespoons black pepper, 1 tablespoon red pepper, 3 tablespoons brown sugar and 1 pint salt. Mix thoroughly and apply dry to each joint all that can be made to adhere. Wrap each joint in two layers of paper and sew muslin cloth around it. Hang in a cool place.

Stuffed Heart

Clean all the lumps of clotted blood out of the heart. Boil until tender, adding scraps of meat to make a rich gravy. When tender, stuff the heart with a dressing made as for roast turkey. Bake until brown and serve with gravy made of the liquor it was boiled in.

Pork Sausage

Season by adding to each 50 lbs. of ground meat—1 lb. salt, 1/8 lb. ground black pepper and a handful of ground coriander seed. Make into cakes, fry in the oven until done. Pack in a stone jar and cover with melted lard. Sausage put up in this way will keep through the summer season and be very fresh when taken out.

Oven Canned Beef

Put nicely cut pieces of beef in jars and on top of each put 1 teaspoon salt, 1/2 teaspoon pepper and a piece of tallow. Place on grate in oven, not touching each other. Only partially tighten lids on jars. Cook for 2 1/2 or 3 hours after it starts boiling in jars. Do not have oven too hot. Remove and seal.

Soup Stock

Boil beef, mutton and veal shanks (or whatever meat you have on hand) together for four hours, watching carefully to remove all scum that will rise; strain; after which it is ready for use. This is a good foundation for all soups.

Don't throw away the less tender outer leaves of cabbage or lettuce. Add them to your favorite soup for a flavor and nutritional boost.

November 24, 1892
*The largest white gobbler from our flock was the center-
piece and main food for our Thanksgiving dinner today. On
the table, there were mounds of fluffy mashed potatoes
heaped high in the bowl with a pool of melted butter on top;
corn smothered in fresh cream; sweet potato slices swim-
ming in butter and sorghum molasses; layers of different
kinds of pickles and preserves laid out on a serving tray;
oven-warm biscuits, and sliced rye bread.*

Turkey Stuffings

Bread Dressing—To 1 quart bread crumbs, add 1
chopped onion, salt, pepper and sage to taste, 1 or 2 beaten
eggs, and fatty meat liquor to moisten.

Oyster Dressing—Mix together 1 quart stale bread
crumbs, 1 pint finely chopped oysters, 1 beaten egg, 2
tablespoons melted butter, 1 teaspoon herbs and milk
enough to moisten.

Baking Powder Biscuits

1 cup flour
2 tblsps. baking powder
1/4 teaspoon salt

1 teaspoon lard
1/2 cup milk

Mix together and pat out to 1 inch thickness. Cut with
biscuit cutter. Bake in a hot oven. This makes 6 to 8 biscuits.

Bruna Bönor

Measure 3 cups beans and sort. Cover beans with cold water and cook for 2 1/2 hours. (After 1 1/4 hours, put 1/4 teaspoon baking soda in it.) When tender, add 1/3 teaspoon cinnamon, 3 tablespoons vinegar, 3 tablespoons molasses, 1/4 cup brown sugar, 1/4 cup white sugar and 1/4 teaspoon salt. Mix 1 tablespoon cornstarch with a little water, then pour slowly into beans. If not thick enough, add more cornstarch.

Baked Onions

Peel and parboil onions for 10 minutes. Make a sauce by melting 2 tablespoons butter and mixing in 4 tablespoons flour. Add a little pepper, 1 teaspoon salt, 2 tablespoons lemon juice, and 2 cups boiling milk. Cook until thick. Put onions in casserole. Pour sauce over onions; cover and bake in slow oven for 1 hour.

Sweet Potatoes

Cut up 1 quart sweet potatoes in squares. Add 1 cup sugar, 1/2 cup water, 4 or 5 whole cloves and a tablespoonful of butter. Let cook until soft, then add 1/2 cup cream and let cook about 5 minutes.

Green Tomato Mince

Grind 1 peck green tomatoes. Drain off juice and add as much water as juice drained off. Add 3 lbs. brown sugar and 2 lbs. raisins. Cook slowly until tomatoes are tender. Add 2 tablespoons each cloves, cinnamon, allspice, salt and 1 cup vinegar. Boil 45 minutes, then add 2 quarts chopped or ground apples. Boil until apples are done. Fine for pies.

Peach Pickles

peeled peaches
2 pints sugar
1 pint vinegar

stick cinnamon
whole cloves

Make syrup in proportion of 2 pints sugar to 1 pint vinegar, amount depending on amount of peaches. Place spices in bag and then cook with peaches in syrup until tender. Seal in jars while hot.

Pickled Pears

Peel pears, leaving stems on. Steam until you can pierce them with a fork. Boil together for five minutes: 1 1/2 lbs. sugar, 1 pint vinegar, 1/2 ounce stick cinnamon and a 1/4 ounce cloves. Skim syrup. Add pears and boil until syrup thickens. Take pears out and place in jars. Boil syrup five minutes longer and pour over pears. Seal while hot.

November 24, 1892

After all the time we spent making the pumpkin pies—scooping out the pumpkin seeds, peeling and cooking the vegetable's innards, mixing the custard and baking the pies—the thick slices overloaded with whipped cream were devoured in minutes.

Pumpkin Pie

1 cup cooked pumpkin   1/2 cup sugar
1/4 cup cream   1/4 teaspoon ginger
3/4 cup milk   2 teaspoons cinnamon
2 eggs   1/4 teaspoon salt

Mix and pour in unbaked pie crust and bake.

Pumpkin Pudding

1 cup cooked pumpkin   1/4 teaspoon cloves
1/2 to 3/4 cup sugar   1/4 teaspoon ginger
2 eggs separated   1 teaspoon vanilla
a pinch of salt   1 cup milk
1/2 teaspoon cinnamon

Mix together all ingredients but egg whites. Beat egg whites until stiff and mix into pumpkin mixture. Pour into pudding dish or into a pie crust and bake.

December 10, 1892
There have been several jackrabbit hunts in the area now
that the ground is covered with snow.

Baked Jack Rabbit

If the rabbit is old, after dressing, parboil for 3 to 5 minutes, adding about 1 teaspoon soda to the hot water, and then drain. Wrap slices of salt pork around the rabbit. This imparts a good flavor and prevents drying out of the meat. Season and dredge well with flour, and put a few bits of butter around the rabbit in the pan, adding a very little water, and about 1 tablespoon vinegar. Baste often. When done, thicken the gravy with a little flour.

December 19, 1892
The Stenfors' six-week-old baby Lillie died yesterday. I
brought over food for their noon meal, but it sits untouched.
The silence in the house was as still as the fields I passed.
Many young deaths have saddened our neighbors this year.

Meat Pie

Bits of leftover meat can be made into pies. Cut the meat in small pieces and mix with gravy. If you have no gravy, make some by frying onions, brown in drippings, and thickening with flour, adding a very little water. Put the meat and gravy in a pudding dish and cover with mashed potatoes an inch thick. Moisten the top slightly with milk, dot with bits of butter and bake until brown. Serve hot.

Barley Soup

——⟩━⟨——

Cook 1/2 cup barley with 1 slice onion in one quart boiling water for 45 minutes. Strain water off and add 1 quart soup stock and cook until tender. Season with salt and pepper and thicken with 1 cup hot cream and 2 egg yolks.

Soup Dumplings

——⟩━⟨——

Mix 1 egg, 1 cup milk and a pinch of salt. Add enough flour to mix stiff enough to drop from spoon. For each cup of flour used, use 1 teaspoon baking powder. Leave meat in kettle and drop the dumplings on top of broth. Cover closely and boil ten minutes.

Noodles

——⟩━⟨——

Beat up one egg. Add salt. Add flour till stiff. Roll thin. Sprinkle flour over dough. Roll up, cut in strips. Let dry. Put into broth of meat. Cook 15-20 minutes.

Potato Soup

——⟩━⟨——

Dice and cook potatoes in salt water until tender. Drain off water and add milk, chopped onion, butter, salt and pepper to taste. Heat until onion is tender.

January 26, 1894
I celebrated my 21st birthday a day early at Sewing Circle.
The hostess served me the first piece of cake and coffee.

Lemon Cake

2 cups butter
4 cups sugar
1 pint sweet milk
5 eggs

7 cups flour
grated rind of one lemon
1/4 lb. citron
5 teaspoons baking powder

Mix and bake.

Lemon Frosting—Melt 1 teaspoon butter with 1 tablespoon flour. Stir in the grated rind of 1 lemon and the juice of 2 lemons with 1 cup sugar, 1 egg and 1/2 cup water. Boil until it thickens and spread between layers of cake. This will taste better if kept a day or two before cake is cut.

Burnt Sugar Cake

Put 1/2 cup sugar on stove in small pan and burn till the smoke is blue, then pour into this 1/4 cup boiling water and boil together for a few minutes. Cream together 1 1/2 cups sugar and 1/2 cup butter. Add 2 egg yolks and beat. Alternately add 1 cup cold water and 2 1/2 cups flour. Put 2 teaspoons baking powder in last 1/2 cup of flour. Lastly, add burnt sugar syrup and fold in 2 stiffly beaten egg whites. Bake.

Frostings and Icings

---→»•«←---

Burnt Sugar Frosting—Boil together 1 1/2 cups brown sugar and 1/4 cup hot water. Pour this on 1 well beaten egg white. Add burnt sugar. Cook very thick and beat until cool.

Chocolate Icing—Boil 1 cup cream, 1 scant cup sugar, 2 small tablespoons flour and 1/4 cocoa together for eight minutes. Stir until cold.

Cream Icing—Boil 1 1/2 cups sugar, 1/2 teaspoon vanilla and 1/3 cup milk together for five minutes. When cool, beat until creamy.

Maple Nut Frosting—Slowly boil 1 cup sweet cream and 2 cups maple sugar for 1/2 to 3/4 of an hour. Remove from fire and let it cool. Stir in 1 cup chopped walnuts and beat until creamy.

Plain Boiled Icing—Cook 1 1/4 cups sugar and 1/3 cup hot water until it threads. Beat 2 egg whites to a stiff froth. Pour syrup on eggs very slowly, as the egg will cook too fast and the mixture will not thicken if done in a hurry. The more the icing is beaten, the thicker and whiter it becomes.

Strawberry Icing—Mix together 1 beaten egg white and 1 cup sugar. Add 1 cup crushed strawberries. Beat together with an egg beater until it is as thick as whipped cream.

Vanilla Frosting—Dissolve 1 tablespoon cornstarch in 1 cup milk. Beat 1 egg well with 1/2 cup sugar and add to milk. Cook until thick, then flavor with 1 teaspoon vanilla.

May 25, 1894
One of the main items on our shopping list today was glass
canning jars. . . . We usually can over 100 quarts of tomatoes
alone, so we use hundreds of jars to preserve enough food
for the whole year.

Catsup

18 ripe tomatoes
4 onions
1 quart vinegar

1 cup sugar
2 green peppers
all kinds of mixed spices

Boil together thoroughly, bottle and seal.

To Salt Down
Whole Ripe Tomatoes

Pack ripe and perfectly sound tomatoes carefully in
large stone jars and pour a very strong brine over them.
Cover tight to keep out air. When you want to use some, take
out the number of tomatoes you want and soak them for 24
hours in cold water. They can then be peeled and sliced, and
will taste as though they have just come from the vines.

December 25, 1894
Christmas didn't seem right with Willie missing from our family circle around the Christmas tree last night. Three weeks ago, we sent him a package of presents and a carefully wrapped tin of Christmas cookies . . .

Christine's Fruit Cake

1 cup butter	1 teaspoon baking powder
2 cups sugar	1 tablespoon cinnamon
1 cup molasses	1 tablespoon nutmeg
1 cup sweet milk	1 lb. raisins
5 cups flour	1 lb. currants
3 eggs	1/2 lb. each citron and nuts

Mix together all ingredients and bake for an hour.

Peanut Brittle

2 cups sugar	1 teaspoon vanilla
1 cup white syrup	1 tablespoon butter
1/2 cup water	1 teaspoon soda
1 lb. shelled peanuts	

Boil sugar, syrup and water 10 minutes, then add peanuts. Let cook until it turns light brown color. Stir often. Add vanilla, butter and soda, stir quickly and turn out on slab to cool. Spread very thin.

April 19, 1895
. . . *Mamma hosted the Women's Missionary Society today. Mamma was very particular about the coffee (two raw eggs to clarify the brew) and food we served for refreshments. Only the best-looking spritz cookies were served.*

Spritz

1 cup butter	2 1/2 cups flour
3/4 cup sugar	1 teaspoon almond extract
2 egg yolks	dash of salt

Mix together. Put into cookie press and squeeze out to make circles or "S" shapes. Bake in hot oven until edges start to turn brown.

Lemon Snaps

1 cup butter	1 tablespoon sour milk
2 cups sugar	the juice of 1/2 a lemon
2 eggs	flour enough to roll out
1 teaspoon soda	

Cream the butter and sugar, add the well-beaten eggs and then the other ingredients. Roll out thin on a floured board, cut in shapes and bake in hot oven. Any other flavor than lemon may be used for the snaps if preferred.

May 19, 1895
One of the women asked for my White Delicate Cake recipe
because it was so good. I pulled out the old ledger book that
I've written recipes in and made her a copy.

White Delicate Cake

2 tablespoons butter
1 1/2 cups sugar
1 teacup sweet milk
7 egg whites
3 cups sifted flour

2 heaping teaspoons
baking powder
1 teaspoon of vanilla,
 lemon or almond extract

Cream butter and sugar, add to it the milk, eggs and extract, then add the flour in which the baking powder is well mixed. Bake and frost.

December 20, 1895
The Rittgers gave a wonderful Christmas party with carol-
ing and games, like spin the bottle. I helped make popcorn
balls, while the men buttered their hands to pull taffy.

Popcorn Balls

Mix 1 pint each of syrup and sugar, 2 tablespoons butter and 1 teaspoon vinegar in a large pan. Cook until the syrup hardens when dropped into cold water. Remove from fire and add 1/2 teaspoon soda dissolved in a tablespoon of hot water. Pour over the popcorn while hot. Mold into balls.

Vinegar Taffy

—————

In a pan mix 1 cup molasses, 1 cup sugar, 2 tablespoons vinegar and 1 tablespoon butter. Boil until a test drop hardens in water. Pull taffy.

Old-Fashioned Butterscotch

—————

2 cups brown sugar   2 tablespoons water
1/2 cup butter   2 tablespoons vinegar
4 tablespoons molasses

Use kettle deep enough to allow for foaming. Cook to the brittle stage. Turn in thin layers in buttered pans, mark into squares and break apart when cold.

Cocoa Fudge

—————

3 cups sugar   4 or 5 tablespoons cocoa
1 cup cream or milk   1 teaspoon vanilla

Mix ingredients in sauce pan. Stir and boil until a few drops makes soft ball when tested in cold water. Cool and stir until creamy. Pour on a buttered plate and cut into pieces.

Homemade Candy

Boil 1 or 2 potatoes, mash and beat until fluffy. Mix with powdered sugar and flavor to taste. Roll thin and spread with peanut butter. Roll as for jelly roll and cut across, or shape and dip in melted chocolate.

Peppermints

1 1/2 cups sugar
6 teaspoons boiling water
1 teaspoon powdered sugar

1/2 teaspoon cream of tartar
1 teaspoon essence
of peppermint

Boil sugar and water to the soft ball state. Remove from heat and add rest of the ingredients. Stir until thick and creamy.

Sea Foam

Boil 2 cups brown sugar and 2/3 cup hot water until a little dropped in cold water will harden. Beat a little at a time into 1 stiffly beaten egg white. Continue beating until spoonful of the mixture will stand in shape when dropped on oiled paper.

March 26, 1896

I delivered eggs to Assaria today so I could buy material for my latest project. Mrs. Mattson asked me to do it.
A bolt of white shirt material for the six boys was easy to pick out, but I looked through the selection more carefully for the girls' dresses. You can always tell who are sisters in a crowd because their dresses are all made from the same material.

Hannah Mattson and her children

November 26, 1896
All the men who have spent the last few weeks snapping corn
congregated around the school stove while we set up the
food on the long plank tables for our Thanksgiving dinner.
It has become the tradition to have a group Thanksgiving
dinner in the schools.

Vanilla Custard

2 1/2 cups boiling milk   1/2 cup sugar
2 eggs, separated   a pinch of salt
2 heaping tbsp. cornstarch   1 teaspoon vanilla

Mix together all ingredients (but hot milk and egg whites), adding a little milk or cream to make a smooth paste. Add to the boiling milk, and cook a little while until thick. Add vanilla after you have removed it from the stove.

You may add 1/2 cup coconut, 1/2 cup dates or 1/2 cup chocolate to the custard.

Pour into a casserole and beat the egg whites with 2 teaspoons sugar. Spread on top. Brown in the oven.

Chocolate Pie

2 cups milk   2 tablespoons cocoa
3/4 cup sugar   1 egg
2 tablespoons cornstarch   salt

Mix dry ingredients and add milk. Add dab of butter. Beat in egg yolk. Cook, stirring. Pour into baked pie shell.

Chocolate Tapioca Pudding

Soak 1/2 cup tapioca in cold water until soft. Drain. Pour on enough boiling water to cover well and cook until clear. Add 1 cup sugar, a bit salt and 1/4 cup cocoa. Mix well. Next, lightly stir in 2 beaten egg whites and 1 teaspoon vanilla. Pour in dish to cool and serve with whipped cream.

Tapjåca Cream

Såk (soak) 4 tablespoons big tapjåca (tapioca) in vatten (water). Then cook in 1 quart of milk until clear. Add 2 beaten egg yolks, 1 cup sugar, 1 tablespoon butter and a speck of salt to tapioca and cook a little. Then fold in the beaten whites into the cooked mixture. Flavor with vanilla.

Cream Puffs

Mix 1 cup water, 1/2 cup butter, 1 cup flour, boil together until it leaves the sides of the pan. When cool, add 3 unbeaten eggs, one at a time, stirring briskly, then drop with a spoon on a well greased baking pan and bake about 30 minutes until a golden brown. Cut a place in top, fill with whipped cream sweetened and flavored. Replace the cover and serve.

May 3, 1897

Since the Lamkins sold their farm to the west of us a few years ago, it's had different families renting the farmstead, mostly English people. Now we have Swedish neighbors again, actually from our church. Peter Oborg and his wife Gunilla, who is a few years younger than me, have moved in this week. . . . They have two little boys, Olof, about two years old, and Luther, who is one.

Peter and Gunilla Oborg

July 2, 1897

We've sweltered in 100 degree temperature every day this last week. The threshing machines are busy, so we celebrated Julia's birthday at noon with a table full of threshers. It was so hot in the house the frosting almost melted off the cake before dinner.

Apple Sauce Cake

1 cup sugar
1/2 cup butter
1 egg
1 1/2 cups apple sauce
2 teaspoons soda

spices
1 cup raisins
1 cup nuts
2 1/4 cups flour

Mix and bake.

Apple Frosting—To 1 cup sugar, add 1 egg, 2 or 3 grated sour apples and the juice and grated rind of one lemon. Boil and stir until it thickens. Cool before spreading on cake.

Chocolate Cake

1 1/2 cups sugar
1/2 cup butter
1/2 cup sour milk
2 eggs

2 cups flour
1/2 cup cocoa mixed in
1/2 cup hot water
1 1/2 teaspoons soda

Bake in loaf or layers in moderate oven until done.

Short Cake

scant cup of sugar
big tablespoon of butter
1 cup water
2 eggs

3 teaspoons baking powder
flavoring
flour for thin dough

Mix, bake and top with icing.

Spice Cake

1 cup brown sugar
1/2 cup sugar
1 cup butter
1 cup sour milk
or buttermilk

2 cups flour
2 eggs
1 each teaspoon soda,
cinnamon and cloves

Bake in layers and ice.

Nut Cake

2 cups sugar
1 cup butter
6 egg whites, beaten stiff
1/4 cup milk

3 cups flour
2 teaspoons baking powder
1 cup nut meats

Mix and bake.

August 8, 1897
*On our way down to the river to fish, we paused a minute
to watch the informal baseball game of the neighborhood
boys on the school grounds.*

Baked Fresh Fish

After thoroughly cleaning fish, let it lie in salted cold
water half an hour, take out and dry with a towel. Butter a
dripping pan, lay the fish in, sprinkle with salt and pepper
inside. Also have a teacupful of dry bread crumbs with butter
the size of an egg. Put bits of butter and crumbs on the
outside of the fish. Pour one pint of boiling water in pan
around the fish, and bake half an hour.

Fiskpudding

2 lbs. raw boneless fish   1/4 cup flour
1 1/2 teaspoons salt   2 cups milk
1/4 teaspoon pepper   3 eggs, separated
1/4 cup butter   melted butter

Chop up fish. Add salt and pepper. Melt butter in
saucepan, stir in flour and cook until it bubbles. Add milk
and cook several minutes over a low heat. Stir some of the
thickened hot sauce into the slightly beaten egg yolks, then
stir into remaining sauce. Add to fish. Beat egg whites until
stiff and fold into first mixture. Turn into casserole dish and
set in a pan containing a little water. Bake in a slow oven
for 1 1/2 hours.

January 11, 1898
Gunilla was about to deliver their newest child. I fixed the little boys some breakfast of milk gravy and rye bread, which they washed down with a big glass of milk. Peter paced the floor while Elsa Theolinda was born.

Milk Gravy

After frying salt pork, take the meat out, add milk to the drippings and heat. Stir in a little flour paste to thicken gravy. Add salt and pepper to taste. Serve gravy over slices of brown bread and salt pork strips.

Waffles

2 cups flour	1 1/2 cups milk
3 teaspoons baking powder	4 tablespoons butter
1/2 teaspoon salt	sugar if wanted
2 eggs	

Mix and bake in waffle iron.

Flannel Cakes

Mix 1 pint flour, well sifted, 2 teaspoons salt, 1 tablespoon butter and 1 pint sour milk. Mix all thoroughly and just before frying, stir in 1/2 teaspoon soda dissolved in a little water. Fry on a hot griddle. Do not have batter too thin.

June 18, 1898
While I was sitting on the back porch snapping beans this afternoon, I could see Peter weaving through the wheat field, stooping now and then to examine a ripening wheat head. . . . During supper Peter said he spied black rust on the wheat stems which means the yield is down. Farming can be so unpredictable.

To Salt Down String Beans

Wash and drain, string and break or cut up beans into small pieces. Pack the beans into a crock in alternate layers with salt, beginning and topping off with a layer of salt. Keep in a moderately warm place so that salt will dissolve and form a brine, which should cover the beans well. Beans and salt may be added from day to day until the jar is full. Then cover inside with a clean cloth, plate or board, and weight down with a clean stone. Be sure that the brine covers the beans. Cover the crock, tie over with cloth or paper, and set away in a cool place.

Canned Green Beans

Cook beans, adding salt to taste. For every 4 quarts of beans, add 1 teacup of vinegar. Cook until tender and can.

When preparing to eat later, soak overnight, then boil twice the next morning to remove the vinegar taste. Add a piece of bacon and a little sugar when cooking for meal.

December 25, 1899
On Christmas day, you put the cookie in the palm of your
hand, make a wish, then tap in the center of the cookie. If
the pepparkakor breaks into three pieces, your wish will
come true. Luck was with me!
Then I found the almond in my serving of Christmas rispud-
ding. Everyone knows that means the finder will marry
within the year.

Pepparkakor

3/4 cup butter
1/2 cup sugar
1/2 cup molasses
1 egg
1 teaspoon soda

3 cups flour
1/2 teaspoon cloves
1 teaspoon cinnamon
and ginger

Mix ingredients. Roll dough thin and cut in shapes.
Bake 8 to 10 minutes until done.

Rice Cream

Beat 4 eggs and add 1 cup of sugar and vanilla extract.
Scald 2 cups of milk or cream, mix with the eggs and sugar,
and cook until thick, stirring constantly. While still hot, add
1 cup of boiled rice. When entirely cold, add 1 cup of
whipped cream, and set to form in a wet mold. This is
delicious served with light cake.

July 17, 1900
This summer as I pull weeds in the garden, ladle boiling currant jelly into scalded jars, . . . I keep thinking this is the last season I'll do this task on this farm.

Currant Jelly

Clean picked currants, put them in a preserving kettle, and let stand on back of range until juices draw. Stir occasionally until skins are broken and then pour into jelly bag, made of cheese cloth or flannel and let drain overnight. To each pint juice, allow 1 pint sugar. Put sugar in oven to heat, put juice over fire, and boil and skim 20 minutes. Add hot sugar, stir until melted, and let boil up again a few minutes, after which remove from fire and fill at once into jelly glasses.

Rhubarb Marmalade

2 quarts rhubarb   1/2 cup raisins, cut fine
1 quart sugar   1/2 cup chopped walnuts
rind and juice of 1 orange

Wash, pare and cut rhubarb into 1/2 inch pieces. Add sugar and let stand overnight. In morning, add other ingredients. Bring to boiling point and simmer until thick. Put up in jars and seal.

As the mantle clock struck 3:30, Pastor began reading the wedding vows from his book. . . . I am now Mrs. Nels Runneberg.

The plank tables and chairs borrowed from the school house were set up on the east lawn of the house for the wedding supper. The last tomatoes I'll ever grow here were served with a bounty of food from our farm: chicken, fresh beef, potatoes, currant jelly on wheat bread. Yesterday Mamma, Carrie and Minnie spent the day making pies and bread in each of their kitchens.

Chicken Cutlets

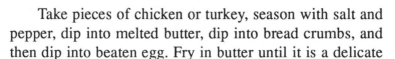

Take pieces of chicken or turkey, season with salt and pepper, dip into melted butter, dip into bread crumbs, and then dip into beaten egg. Fry in butter until it is a delicate brown.

Beef Loaf

3 lbs. of good lean beef   salt and pepper
3 eggs, well beaten   1 teacup water
6 large crackers, rolled fine 1 tablespoon butter

Mix well and mold into a loaf. Bake 1 1/2 hours, basting occasionally. When cold, slice thin.

Scalloped Potatoes

Peel and slice potatoes thin. Put a layer of slices in a tin basin. Sprinkle with pepper, salt, a little flour and a small piece of butter. Keep layering slices and seasonings until the basin is almost full. Then fill the basin half full with sweet milk. Bake half an hour.

Apple Pie

Line a well greased pie tin with pie dough and fill up with apple slices, 4 tablespoons sugar and a little butter and nutmeg. Cover with an upper curst. Then pour cold water over crust, allowing the water to run off. Put in a hot oven. After it is nicely browned, cover with another pie tin and bake one hour at reduced heat.

Oatmeal Raisin Bread

Soak 2/3 cup chopped raisins in 2 cups cold water for 1 hour. Then let come to boiling point, pour over 1 cup rolled oats, cover and let stand for 1 hour. Add 1 tablespoon butter, 1 1/2 teaspoons salt, 1/4 cup brown sugar, 1/2 yeast cake dissolved in 1/2 cup water. Beat, add 4 1/2 cups flour. Let rise in bowl until very light, then beat again and turn into greased bread pans. When light, bake about 1 hour.

September 21, 1900

This week we've stayed on the farm. . . . While Nels helped Peter, I packed our wedding gifts and my belongings for the trip to Iowa.

One of Mamma's presents, "from the farm" as she put it, was several cases of canned fruit, vegetables and jelly that we put up this summer. . . . Whenever I open up a jar to use, I'll close my eyes and see the tree or garden row it came from.

Strawberry Preserves

Boil 1 quart berries and 2 tablespoons vinegar for 3 minutes. Then add 4 cups sugar. Boil 7 minutes. Then pour into an earthen crock, and let stand until the next day. Put in glasses with a paraffin seal on top. Cherries may be done this way also.

Peach Preserves

Peel 1 quart well ripened peaches and cut into small pieces. Mix with 1 quart sugar and let stand overnight. In the morning, add 1 teaspoon cinnamon and boil for 15 to 20 minutes.

__October 1, 1900__
I rose early this morning, leaving Nels in bed. I wanted to walk around the farm one more time . . . From the top of the hill I watched the sun rise and heard the world awaken. Mamma . . . with tears in her own eyes, said, "You will be homesick for us and this farm, but my prayers and your book of memories will help you remember your life here. Go start your new life with your husband. Your prairie is waiting."

The homestead

Peter and Kajsa Runeberg and children

About the Author

Linda K. Hubalek

A door may close in your life, but a window will open instead.

Linda Hubalek knew years ago that she wanted to write a book someday, but it took a major move in her life to find her new career in writing.

Hubalek's chance came unexpectedly when her husband was transferred from his job in the Midwest, to the West Coast. Hubalek had to sell her wholesale floral business and find a new career.

Homesick for her family and the farmland of the Midwest, she turned to writing about what she missed, and the inspiration was kindled to write about her Swedish ancestors and the land they homesteaded.

Even though the story of her family is in her book, Hubalek found the most information about Kajsa Svensson Runeberg, the Swedish woman who homesteaded the farm where Hubalek grew up. Even though Kajsa was not a direct relative of Hubalek's, Kajsa and her descendants have always played a significant role in her life.

After much research and writing, Hubalek's first book, *Butter in the Well*, was published. People were fascinated with the pioneer stories of the immigrant homesteader and asked, "What happened to the family on the farm?" What resulted was Hubalek's second book, *Prärieblomman*, this book, *Egg Gravy*, and the forthcoming book, *Looking Back*.

Kajsa Runeberg in front of her house

Swedish Glossary

biggert: Swedish-English name for meat dish
bruna bönor: brown beans
fader: father
fiskpudding: fish pudding
fruktsoppa: dried fruit cooked into a soup
God Jul: Merry Christmas
kaffebröd: coffee bread
kisslings: Swedish-English word for almond cookie
knäckebröd: crackers
kringlor: sweet pastry
kräm: grape juice sauce
Julafton: Christmas Eve
lutfisk: dried stockfish, soaked, then cooked
moder: mother
ostkaka: a custard dessert or cheesecake
palt: blood pudding
pepparkakor: ginger cookies
plättar: thin pancakes
potatiskorv: potato sausage
prärieblomman: prairie flower
rispudding: cooked rice pudding
sillsallad: beet and herring salad
skorpor: dried sweet bread
smörbakelser: butter cookies
smörgåsbord: variety of foods served buffet style
spritz: a delicate butter cookie
sylta: head cheese
tapjåca: tapioca *(*correct Swedish spelling: *tapioka)*
tack så mycket: thank you very much

Index

the *Butter in the Well* series

"...could well be the most endearing 'first settler' account ever told. Once a reader start the books, they are compelled to keep reading to see what will happen next on the isolated prairie homestead. Not to be missed!"—Capper's Books

Butter in the Well
Read the endearing account of Kajsa Svensson Runeberg, a young immigrant wife who recounts how she and her family built up a farm on the native prairie.
Quality soft book • $9.95 • ISBN 1-886652-00-7 • 6 x 9 • 144 pages
Abridged audio cassette • $9.95 • ISBN 1-886652-04-X • 90 minutes

Prärieblomman
This tender, touching diary continues the saga of the family through the daughter, Alma, as she blossoms into a young woman.
Quality soft book • $9.95 • ISBN 1-886652-01-5 • 6 x 9 • 144 pages
Abridged audio cassette • $9.95 • ISBN 1-886652-05-8 • 90 minutes

Egg Gravy
Everyone who's ever treasured a family recipe or marveled at the special touches that Mother added to her cooking, will enjoy this collection of recipes and wisdom from the homestead family.
Quality soft book • $9.95 • ISBN 1-886652-02-3 • 6 x 9 • 136 pages

Looking Back
During the final week on the land she homesteaded, Kajsa reminisces about the growth and changes she experienced during her 51 years on the farm. Don't miss this heart touching finale!
Quality soft book • $9.95 • ISBN 1-886652-03-1 • 6 x 9 • 140 pages

Butter in the Well Note cards— Three full-color designs per package featuring the family and farm.
***Homestead Note* cards**—This full-color design shows the original homestead.
Either style of note card —$4.95/ set. Each set contains 6 cards and envelopes in a clear vinyl pouch. Each card: 5 1/2 x 4 1/4.
Postcards— One full-color design of homestead. $3.95 for a packet of 12.

Information on how to order these items are on the back side of this page.

Order Form

Butterfield Books

2380 South Waco Court
Aurora, CO 80013
(303) 752-4304
Fax (303) 752-1269

SEND TO:

Name _____

Address _____

City _____

State _____ Zip _____

Phone # _____

☐ Check enclosed for entire amount payable to
Butterfield Books

☐ Visa ☐ MasterCard

Card # ☐☐☐☐ ☐☐☐☐ ☐☐☐☐ ☐☐☐☐

Exp Date ☐☐ ☐☐

ISBN #	TITLE	QTY	UNIT PRICE	TOTAL
1-886652-00-7	Butter in the Well		9.95	
1-886652-01-5	Prärieblomman		9.95	
1-886652-02-3	Egg Gravy		9.95	
1-886652-03-1	Looking Back		9.95	
1-886652-04-X	**Cassette:** Butter in the Well		9.95	
1-886652-05-8	**Cassette:** Prärieblomman		9.95	
	Note cards: Butter in the Well		4.95	
	Note cards: Homestead		4.95	
	Postcards: Homestead		3.95	
	Shipping & Handling: per address ($2.00 for first item. Each additional item .50)			
			CO residents add 7.55% Tax	
			Total	

Signature (or call to place your order)_____ Date_____

Order four books or cassettes, and receive a package of note cards free!

Order the complete set of books, or finish up the series for someone special. Just tell us who to send them to, and your gift will be shipped directly to the receiver with a card enclosed saying it is from you. If this is for a birthday or Christmas gift, please specify, and give us an approx. date you wish the books to arrive.

Order Form

Butterfield Books

2380 South Waco Court
Aurora, CO 80013
(303) 752-4304
Fax (303) 752-1269

SEND TO:

Name _____

Address _____

City _____

State _____ Zip _____

Phone # _____

☐ Check enclosed for entire amount payable to
Butterfield Books

☐ Visa ☐ MasterCard

Card # ☐☐☐☐ ☐☐☐☐ ☐☐☐☐ ☐☐☐☐

Exp Date

ISBN #	TITLE	QTY	UNIT PRICE	TOTAL
1-886652-00-7	Butter in the Well		9.95	
1-886652-01-5	Prärieblomman		9.95	
1-886652-02-3	Egg Gravy		9.95	
1-886652-03-1	Looking Back		9.95	
1-886652-04-X	**Cassette:** Butter in the Well		9.95	
1-886652-05-8	**Cassette:** Prärieblomman		9.95	
	Note cards: Butter in the Well		4.95	
	Note cards: Homestead		4.95	
	Postcards: Homestead		3.95	
	Shipping & Handling: per address ($2.00 for first item. Each additional item .50)			
			CO residents add 7.55% Tax	
			Total	

Signature (or call to place your order)_____ Date_____

Order four books or cassettes, and receive a package of note cards free!

Order the complete set of books, or finish up the series for someone special. Just tell us who to send them to, and your gift will be shipped directly to the receiver with a card enclosed saying it is from you. If this is for a birthday or Christmas gift, please specify, and give us an approx. date you wish the books to arrive.